Contents

Acknowledgement 4
Chapter I. A Turbulent World 8
1.1 The Major Economic Crises 14
Great Depression 15
The Suez Crisis 18
The International Debt Crisis 20
1.2 The World Wars 22
1.3 The Cold War 24
1.4 The Pandemics and Covid-19 29
1.5 Russo-Ukrainian War 32
1.6 The Armed Racing 35

Chapter II. The Global Organizations…………......………41
2.1 The United Nation 42
2.2 World Trade Organization 47
2.3 The Shanghai Cooperation Organization 52
The Roles of Shanghai Cooperation Organization 55
One of SCO's fundamental priorities is to stop the trafficking of illegal drugs 64
Economic Growth as a Tool for Preventing the Development of New Security Challenges and Threats 65

As a Preventive Measure against Security Threats, Cultural Dialogue 67

2.4 The NATO 68

2.5 The BRICS 76

BRICS's Developments 79

2.6 The ASEAN Organization 84

Chapter III. Future of Economic Progress...................**84**

3.1 Agricultural Revolution 90

3.2 Industrial Revolutions 94

First Industrial Revolution 95

Second Industrial Revolution 95

Third Industrial Revolution 96

Fourth Industrial Revolution 97

3.3 Innovation and Modern Technology 98

3.4 International Trade and Cooperation 102

3.5 The Better World and Better Government 109

Chapter Iv. The Global Goals for Sustainable Development 110

4.1 Life's Lessons from the US Navy Seal 119

4.2 The Declining of Russia 125

4.3 What to Watch for in 2023? 129

4.4 Four Things to Review in 2022 132

4.5 Southeast Asia Aspirations for the Future EV Hub 140

Chapter V. Conclusion and Recommendations…….....….174

Acknowledgement

This book is a very extraordinary work. It provides deep analysis on economic and global issues. The book traces the global economic crisis in world history, and it also explains the major confrontations and world wars and the cost of global distractions. Importantly, the book also gives you the basic ideas of how to achieve sustainable development and better government. In addition, the book also predicts the future of economic progress and some major events facing the world.

I am able to complete this incredible effort due of the steadfast support I have received from my loved ones, ministers, councilors, and wife. Dedicating their entire lives to establishing a good family and making a positive impact on society, my late father, Victor Liew Ming Kong, and my most admired mother, Mary Tham Yuk Lan, deserve my deepest gratitude. They were so incredible and amazing to me. I cannot say how lucky I am to be the son. And there aren't enough words to express how grateful I am for their kindness, care, love, and dedication. Without your sacrifices, nothing in my life would have been possible. Nothing I say could really express how much I appreciate you. Nothing I do could fully describe how grateful I am to you. You two are without a doubt the best parents ever.

I also want to express my sincere gratitude to my brother, Clement Liew, who has always stood with me and helped me no matter what. My brother always encourage and inspire me to be better and better as much as I can be. Despite the fact that he has the busiest life, helping society and taking care of his family, he still tries to be my best brother by encouraging and giving advice.

My sincere gratitude also goes out to Cynthia Joyce Petrus, my wonderful and lovely wife, for her patience and spiritual support, encouragement, caring, love, and trying her best to be my best partner in life. She does not only support me in pursuing my dream but also helping me to reach it. Her dedication and commitment plus kindness and comparison are the most crucial factors in my success. I love you so much, my dearest wife.

Without the ongoing support and advice of my esteemed minister, YB. Datuk Seri Panglima Dr. Jeffrey G. Kitingan (JP),

Deputy Chief Minister I of Sabah and Minister of Agriculture and Fisheries of Sabah, Member of Parliament P.180 for Keningau , I would not be able to complete my task or reach my goal. He places his trust in me and provides me the chance to serve the people and the country. He always shows me the good example and dedication to serve the country and the people. He has medicated most of his lifetimes in serving the country and the people.

My thankfulness also would like to extend to my best friend Saldivilla Wences, parliamentary development officer P.180 keningau. I would like to say thank you for being a good friend by sharing knowledge and experience and helping each other. I couldn't have asked for a better friendship than you in terms of real friendship. Remarkably, to become a councillor, I wish to thank Sir Alexius Kiob, Community Development Leaders (PPM) N.39 Tambunan for his good will in guiding me to ministers and members of the council. My sincere and special thanks would be extended to Madam Arlinsia Agang, Secetery of politician to the Deputy Chief Minister I of Sabah for giving me advice, support, guidance, and motivation. I also have learned many things from the former district officer of Tambunan, Sir Jumain Abdul Ghani, such as administrative affairs, management, and development. I would like to acknowledge with gratitude his contribution.

Last but not least, thank you to my friends, instructors, lecturers, and coworkers, who I am unable to name individually. I appreciate you thinking of me as your friend and treating me properly as a decent employee. I sincerely hope you will find this book helpful, both for you and for our society. I want to thank you all once more from the bottom of my heart. I'm hoping the best for you.

Preface

Our world is a global market. Your mobile phone may have been produced in US or Korea. It's possible that the clothing you wear was designed in Italy and made in China. It's possible that the toys you offer children are from India. You may be driving a car made in Korea, Germany, or Japan. Crude oil from Saudi Arabia, Mexico, or Nigeria may be refined into the gasoline in the tank. The watch you wear may be exported from France. Everything you see in the local supermarkets are exported worldwide as the result of global trade and business.

In order to satisfy a need or desire for products or services, people engage in international trade, which involves the exchange of capital, goods, and services across national boundaries. The buying and selling of goods and services between businesses in several nations is referred to as international trade. On the global market, commodities such as consumer products, raw materials, food, and machinery are all purchased and sold. The money you get and pay to your employees come from the export or import of global commerce.

International trade, whose volume has increased significantly over the past few decades, binds us all together.

Through commerce, nations can access commodities and services that might not otherwise be accessible domestically and grow their markets. Market competition has increased as a result of global trade. This ultimately leads to more competitive pricing, which lowers the cost of the final product for the consumer. The expansion of the world economy was largely due to international trade. Global events have an effect on prices in the global economy as well as supply and demand.

In reality, throughout the second part of the nineteenth century, the integration of global markets was quite significant. In fact, 1869, the year the Union Pacific railroad and the Suez Canal were finished, is a good choice if one wishes to pinpoint the start of a truly global economy. Steamships and railroads had established entirely worldwide markets for standardized goods like wheat and wool by the eve of the First World War.

Early in the 20th century, this initial globalization wave came to an abrupt halt. The First World War broke up numerous commercial ties. Many countries made the erroneous decision to cut back on international trade during the Great Depression of the 1930s in an effort to stabilize their own economies. International trade was severely hampered by World War II. After World War II, the world's money and trade flows slowly began to recover. Global economic forces did not resume their pre-World War I importance in relation to the size of the world economy until the early 1980s.

At the end of the Cold War, International trades in international economics has been developed rapidly and dramatically. It has shaped the international environment and international standards of living and it has lift up several countries out of poverty. International trade and international economy have become the leading engines of the global economics. International Financial flows, International trades, International organizations, International Bank and business Networks, aid and technical assistance to developing countries, and many others are the tools of international economy and international trade.

In this book, I try to trace back all major economic crises and major historical events to help analyzing to understand the global economy and international trade better. Three factors influenced my decision to write this book: Firstly, I am a businessman, and I have earned a doctorate in business administration. International trade, in my experience and observation, is the most important factor in developing countries and modernizing everything. So I write a book to promote people's awareness about the significance of business in promoting social welfare and National Economic growth.

Secondly, I want to share my experience and knowledge with people about how international trade and economy have developed and what their perspectives will be. To help people understanding better about global economy and trade, I have traced back the causes of risings and declining in international economy and trades and in the global history. These factors are the proofs and evidence help us avoid repeating same mistakes. I strongly believe that this book is a good advisor telling you what the right causes of economic sustainable growth are.

Finally as a government official, I have strong responsibility to research and learn more about international trade and economy to have shaping the future of my economic growth and helping the future generations to get a better life. Without understanding international trade and business, it would be extremely dangerous for us to compete for economic growth on the edge of uncertainty. It is also our obligation and responsibility to educate our children and others about international trade and economics. It is the best way for us to prepare for the future of our economic growth.

In writing this book, I do not care about the profit that I will make. But I do care if our children and the readers will understand better about international economy and trade. In this book, I am strongly dedicated to my motherland of Malaysia and the people of the world. I hope that all of the readers will gain knowledge and ideas to help them improve their economic development and achieve sustainable development. What we all really want is a more peaceful and prosperous world that we want to live in.

January 30, 2023

Adjunct Professor Dr. James Liew Tze Vun

Chapter I. A Turbulent World

A world war is an international conflict in which most or all of the major powers of the world are involved. Although historians have also referred to other global conflicts as world wars, such as the Cold War and the War on Terror, the term "world war" is traditionally reserved for two major international conflicts that took place during the first half of the 20th century, World War I (1914–1918) and World War II (1939–1945).

In additions the world also have faced many serious Global economics crisis. Over the past seven decades, there have been four worldwide recessions: in 1975, 1982, 1991, and 2009. Each of these periods saw a decline in the yearly real per capita global gross domestic product, which was accompanied by a deterioration of other important global economic activity indices. The worldwide recessions caused serious economic and financial disruptions in many nations throughout the world and were highly synchronized on a global scale. The worldwide recession of 2009, which was brought on by the global financial crisis, was by far the most severe and well-timed of the four recessions. Advanced economies took the burden of the recession because they were the hub of the issue.

1.1 The Major Economic Crises

There are always two opposite sides of nature. The nature as Chinese philosophers described as Yin and Yang. Analogously, the global economy has also gone through its Yin and Yang. There have been many eras in which global growth has reached its zenith. And there have been many times when the worst global economic crises affected the financial and manufacturing industries and caused catastrophes for millions of lives. In this article, we examine the major historical economic crises and their causes. The purposes of studying economic crises are to avoid repeated mistakes and to orient towards sustainable and healthy growth. The worst does not mean that one has never made any mistakes, but the worst is making repeated ones.

The world would have hundreds times wealthier than present-day if world leaders would not have caused major harmful decisions. There has been over hundreds economic crises globally for over last 100 years. Among them, the major global economic crises are worth considering preventing them from reoccurring.

Great Depression

Between 1929 and 1939, the Great Crisis was a devastating global economic recession that started with a significant drop in stock values in the United States. The economic pandemic began about September 4, 1929, and was widely publicized on Black Tuesday, October 29, 1929, when the stock market crashed. The economic catastrophe spread over the world, affecting countries to varied degrees, with the Great Depression affecting the majority of countries. The Great Slump was the twentieth century's largest, worst, and most extensive anxiety, and it is often used as an example of a severe worldwide economic downturn.

The American economy grew by 42 percent in the 1920s, while stock market prices surged by 218 percent in seven years, from 1922 to 1929. No country had ever seen a stock market bubble that drew millions of Americans into speculative trading. No one saw the share-market implosion approaching, and until it struck, Americans trusted in continuous prosperity. The fall of the American stock markets in 1929 had no sensible explanation.

Thousands of investors lost about $30 billion in a single day. Following the stock market crash of 1929 in the United States, a number of banking crisis erupted in Europe in 1931, causing financial contagion to the U. S., the Great Britain, and finally the rest of the world, ushering in the Great Depression. The Great Depression, which ran from 1929 to 1939, was the world's worst economic slump. Human misery was the most severe impact of the Great Depression. The world's productivity and living standards plummeted dramatically in a short period of time. In the early 1930s, one-fourth of the labor force in industrialized countries was unemployed.

Global GDP decreased by 15% between 1929 and 1932. In contrast, during the Great Recession, global GDP declined by less than 1% from 2008 to 2009. Personal income, prices, tax revenues, profits, and prices all dropped dramatically in both rich and poor countries. International trade decreased by more than half, and unemployment in the United States soared to 23%, with other countries reaching 33%.

By 1933, 15 million Americans had lost their jobs, 20,000 businesses had perished, and the majority of American banks had collapsed. 35 countries had renounced gold and gold-exchange standards by 1933. In 1932, the value of exports decreased by 35% in France, 40% in Germany, and 33% in the United States, compared to 7% in the United Kingdom and 19% in Canada. Industrial activity showed economic recovery in the United Kingdom, France, and Germany, with the United States experiencing a significant industrial upturn in April and May 1933.

President Franklin D. Roosevelt's "New Deal" ushered in substantial economic reforms in the United States, establishing the groundwork for the American welfare state — federal unemployment benefits, more industry regulation, legal worker protections, and the Social Security program. The "New Deal" was the first stage in the United States' strong recovery from the Great Depression, and it marked the start of the country's ascension to unchallenged "leader of the free world." However, some countries had continued to suffer till the Second World War broke out.

The Suez Crisis

The Suez Canal Company was nationalized by Egypt on July 26, 1956. On October 29, 1956, France, Israel, and the United Kingdom began a combined military operation, with Israel entering Sinai. During the two-month military action, a financial crisis arose amid the chaos and uncertainty. All four countries sought financial help from the IMF very immediately. Egypt's independence, Israel's survival as a nation, and a catastrophic blow to Britain's Victorian dreams was all political outcomes. The Suez Canal was blocked for six months, causing trade diversion, cost hikes, and supply delays that impacted all four countries' current account balances.

The Egyptian president, Gamal Abdel Nasser, nationalized the Suez Canal on July 26, 1956, precipitating an international crisis in the Middle East. The Suez Canal Company, which was controlled by French and British interests, owned the canal. In response to Egypt's expanding relations with communist Czechoslovakia and the Soviet Union, the United States and the United Kingdom decided not to fund the construction of the Aswan High Dam as promised. Nasser responded to the decision by proclaiming military rule in the Canal Zone and seized control of the Suez Canal Company, stating that revenue earned from ships traveling through the canal will indeed pay for the dam's construction within 5 years.

Nasser was feared by Britain and France to stop the canal, cutting off petroleum flows from the Persian Gulf to Western Europe. As diplomatic attempts to resolve the crisis faltered, the United Kingdom and France secretly planned military action to reclaim control of the canal and, if possible, to overthrow Nasser. They found a willing ally in Israel, whose animosity toward Egypt had been heightened by Nasser's blockade of the Tiran Straits. Ten Israeli brigades invaded Egypt on October 29, 1956, and proceeded to the canal, destroying Egyptian soldiers. Implementing their strategy, Britain and France requested that Israeli and Egyptian forces leave the canal, and they indicated that they would intervene to impose an UN-ordered cease-fire.

The Canal Zone was taken over by British and French soldiers on November 5 and 6. This initiative was immediately met with domestic opposition at the UN resolutions backed by the US. Nasser was victorious and a hero for Arab and Egyptian nationalism after the Suez Crisis. Israel did not acquire access to the canal, but it did reclaim its shipping rights in the Tiran Straits. Britain and France, on the other hand, suffered a significant loss of influence in the Middle East as a result of the incident.

It really is easy to forget history in the midst of a whirl of movement. Because of the changes it triggered in political relations, this brief burst is unanimously viewed as a crisis. Suez was a financial disaster for the United Kingdom, France, Egypt, Israel, and interrupted the global trade. The Suez Canal catastrophe has thrown the worldwide supply chain into turmoil. The billions dollars were cost in the meaningless war.

The International Debt Crisis

The 1980s will almost likely be remembered as the decade of the international debt crisis, a time of dragging the global economics to severely injure. Much has been developed to remedy such issues since the crisis began, but a comprehensive solution to the indebtedness issues has proved elusive. The causes can be traced back to 1970s and 1980s economic policies and development decisions. OPEC countries put much of their new cash in commercial banks when the Organization of Petroleum Exporting Countries (OPEC) tripled the price of oil in 1973. In order to raise capital for their new funds, banks made loans to developing countries, frequently quickly and without closely monitoring how the money was spent.

Some of the funds were used for programs that did not serve the poor, such as armaments, failing or ineffective large-scale development projects, and private projects that benefited government officials and a small elite. Meanwhile, as inflation in the United States increased, the government enacted extraordinarily tight monetary policies, which resulted in a dramatic rise in interest rates and a global recession. Creditors' imprudent lending, debtors' mismanagement, and the global recession all led to the debt crisis of the early 1980s.

The global recession hit developing countries the hardest. The high cost of fuel, hefty interest rates, and dwindling exports made repaying their debts increasingly difficult. Commercial banks and bilateral creditors attempted to address the situation for the rest of the decade and into the 1990s by rescheduling loans and, in some circumstances, granting some debt relief.

Despite these efforts, many of the world's poorest countries' debts are still far beyond their ability to repay.

1.2 The World Wars

The assassination of Archduke Franz Ferdinand of Austria was the beginning of the World War I, also known as the Great War, in 1914. His assassination sparked a war that raged across Europe until 1918. The Central Powers (Germany, Austria-Hungary, Bulgaria, and the Ottoman Empire) fought Great Britain, France, Russia, Italy, Romania, Canada, Japan, and the United States during the conflict (the Allied Powers). World War I had seen extreme levels of death and destruction and destruction, owing to new military technologies and the atrocities of battlefields.

More than 16 million people, both soldiers and civilians, had died by the time the war ended and the Allied Powers declared victory. Economic casualties were numerous in this conflict. In terms of economics, the World War I —which cost approximately $208 billion to fight—caused the twentieth century's greatest global depression. With the exception of the United States, debts accumulated by all major combatants stalked the postwar economic world. The unemployment rate had reached an all-time high. Inflation drove up the cost of living dramatically, particularly in Weimar Germany, where hyperinflation caused a loaf of bread to cost 428 billion marks by December 1923. A period of relative economic prosperity ended abruptly after the First World War, and two decades of economic misery followed.

World War II was the world's second war, lasting from 1939 to 1945. It was the deadliest conflict in human history, involving the majority of the world's countries. The rise of fascism in Europe was one of the major causes of World War II. Fascism is a political system in which a dictator has complete power.

World War II, also known as the Second World War, was a global conflict that lasted from 1939 to 1945. The Axis powers—Germany, Italy, and Japan—and the Allies—France, the United Kingdom, the United States, the Soviet Union, and, to a lesser extent, China—were the main combatants. In many ways, the war was a continuation of the conflicts left unresolved by World War I, following a tense 20-year pause. World War II was the bloodiest and largest war in history, with 40–50 million deaths.

War has always been an expensive exercise, and World War II was by far the most costly war in history. The war's economic cost has altered the world's power structure, which has had a significant impact. Despite the fact that World War Two lasted less than four years, it was the most expensive war in history. The war cost over $4 trillion when adjusted for inflation in today's dollars.

1.3 The Cold War

After World War II, the tense alliance that had helped the United States, Great Britain, and the Soviet Union defeat Nazi Germany started to fall apart, giving rise to an ongoing political conflict between the two superpowers and their allies that came to be known as the Cold War, a term that was independently coined by English writer George Orwell and American presidential adviser Bernard Baruch.

The only two superpowers left standing after World War II were the United States and the Soviet Union. In the late 1940s and early 1950s, while the United States was implementing the Marshall Plan to aid in the recovery of the economies and democracies of Western Europe, the U.S.S.R. was establishing communist regimes in Eastern Europe and tightly controlling them. The North Atlantic Treaty Organization (NATO), led by the United States, and the Warsaw Pact, led by the Soviet Union, were two military alliances that competed by the mid of the 1950s. The Soviet bloc gained another powerful ally in the People's Republic of China with the communists' victory in the Chinese Civil War in 1949.

The two sides fought an intellectual war for the hearts and minds of the rest of the globe, especially the decolonized countries of the so-called Third World, throughout the course of the following four decades and beyond. When one side was up against forces sponsored by the other, or when conflicts were waged indirectly through surrogates, the rivalry would occasionally become hot (most notably the Korean and Vietnam wars). During the Cuban missile crisis in 1962, the world was on the verge of nuclear war with both sides possessing nuclear weapon arsenals.

Then, as they raced one another to build up their arsenals of nuclear weapons while attempting to negotiate disarmament, the Soviet Union and the United States threatened the Earth with enormous catastrophe. The U.S.S.R. and the U.S. competed on every field imaginable, from the race to space to the sprint for Olympic finish lines, in an effort to convince the world of the supremacy of their two ideologies—Soviet communism and American democratic capitalism. Propaganda, influence-peddling, and generous military and financial support were also among their weapons. The Soviet Union and its bloc were broken apart in the beginning of the 1990s, bringing an end to the Cold War, though the reasons for this are still up for debate.

Following World War II, President Truman raised the containment of communism as a worldwide strategy and rejected the implications of the Soviet Union's triumph over the Nazis. By the Cold War, the Soviet Union had recovered from weariness and had made significant advances such as the atomic bomb and the space program before collapsing. China became powerful as a result of American efforts aimed at limiting Communism. Additionally, the Cold War hindered peace agreements between East and West and locked the world into its immediate postwar positions. Since 1945, the United States has invested enough money on the Cold War to heal many sick societies, endangering the stability of our economy.

Millions of people died in the superpowers' proxy battles around the world, most notably in Southeast Asia, in addition to the casualties among uniformed forces. With the conclusion of the Cold War, the majority of proxy conflicts and local conflict funding ended. After the Cold War, there was a significant decrease in the frequency of interstate wars, ethnic wars, revolutionary wars, as well as refugees and disputes between the leaders of the afflicted countries.

Nation-states were still feeling the aftereffects of the Cold War economically and socially a century later. For instance, after 1991, Russia drastically reduced its military budget, which led to a fall in the military-industrial sector of the Soviet Union. Millions of workers were made unemployed as a result of this disassembly, which had an impact on Russia's economy and military.

Russia experienced a financial crisis in the 1990s after starting a number of economic reforms. During the Great Depression, the Russian recession was more debilitating than those felt in the US and Germany. Despite the fact that general Russian living standards declined following the Cold War, the economy continued to develop significantly after 1995. It was shown in early 2005 that the economy has stabilized at its per capita GDP levels from 1989.

After it ended, the Cold War continued to have an impact on world politics. The collapse of the Soviet Union put an end to the Cold War and created what is now usually regarded as a unipolar world, with the United States as the lone surviving hyperpower. However, many other emerging states have significant global impact and are unquestionably superpowers. After World War II, the United States' political role was shaped by the Cold War.

With 50 military alliances and 1.5 million troops stationed overseas in 117 nations by 1989, the world has formalized a commitment to a sizable, perpetual military-industrial complex and massive military sponsorship of science. Additionally, the

US played a major role in the establishment of Peacetime Defense and the arms industry, both of which were mentioned in President Dwight Eisenhower's parting speech.

Nearly 100,000 Americans lost their lives in the Korean and Vietnam Wars, while the US spent between 8 and 9 trillion dollars on its military throughout the Cold War.

1.4 The Pandemics and Covid-19

The COVID-19 pandemic, sometimes referred to as the coronavirus pandemic, is an ongoing global disease outbreak brought on by the coronavirus 2 that causes severe acute respiratory syndrome (SARS-CoV-2). In December 2019, an epidemic in the Chinese city of Wuhan led to the discovery of the new virus. There were futile attempts to contain it, which allowed the virus to spread to other parts of Asia and eventually the entire world. On January 30, 2020, and March 11, 2020, respectively, the World Health Organization (WHO) labeled the outbreak a pandemic and a public health emergency of international concern. The pandemic was one of the deadliest in history as of 11 January 2023, with more than 665 million illnesses and 6.71 million confirmed deaths.

Although COVID-19 symptoms can range from being undetectable to fatal, fever, dry cough, and exhaustion are the most frequent ones. Elderly people and those with specific underlying medical disorders are more likely to have severe sickness. When humans breathe in air contaminated by droplets and other small airborne particles carrying the virus, COVID-19 is spread. These can be breathed over longer distances, especially indoors, but the risk is greatest when people are close together. Transmission can also happen if contaminated fluids go in the mouth, nose, or eyes, or, less frequently, if they come in contact with contaminated surfaces. Numerous strains (variants) with various levels of virulence and infectivity have been created as a result of mutations.

Since December 2020, the COVID-19 vaccination has been authorized and widely supplied in a number of nations. In 185 nations and territories between December 8, 2020, and December 8, 2021, COVID-19 vaccines reportedly avoided an additional 14.4 million to 19.8 million deaths, according to a research published in June 2022. The use of masks, social seclusion, increased ventilation and air filtration, isolation of individuals who have been exposed, and quarantining those who are infected are further preventive measures that are advised. Symptom management and new antiviral medications are included in treatments. Travel restrictions, lockdowns, business closures, workplace hazard controls, quarantines, testing programs, and contact tracing of the infected are examples of public health mitigation measures. These measures, along with treatments, help to bring the pandemic under control and eventually to an end.

Around the world, the pandemic has caused significant social and economic disruption, including the biggest global recession since the Great Depression. Supply chain breakdowns led to widespread shortages of supplies, particularly food. In terms of economic calculation, the total cost to the global economy caused by COVID-19 is more than $15 trillion. Pollution dropped by an incredible amount when human activity decreased. Throughout 2020 and 2021, many jurisdictions closed all or part of their educational institutions and public spaces, and numerous events were postponed or cancelled. Political tensions have increased as a result of false information spreading through social media and the media. The pandemic has brought up questions of racial and geographic discrimination, health fairness, and how to strike a balance between the needs of the public health and the rights of individuals.

1.5 Russo-Ukrainian War

Since February 2014, Russia and Ukraine have been at war with one other (separatists in Ukraine). After the Revolution of Dignity in Ukraine, Russia annexed Crimea and backed pro-Russian rebels fighting Ukrainian government forces in the Donbas region. During the first eight years of the conflict, there were also maritime incidents, cyber-attacks, and heightened political tensions. The battle significantly intensified in February 2022 when Russia began an invasion of Ukraine on a large scale.

Viktor Yanukovych, the pro-Russian leader of Ukraine, was sacked from power in the early months of 2014 as a result of the pro-European Euromaidan and the Revolution of Dignity. Pro-Russian rioting started to spread throughout eastern and southern Ukraine not long after Yanukovych was overthrown and forced into exile in Russia. At the same time, unmarked Russian troops entered the Ukrainian province of Crimea and seized control of key locations and infrastructure, including administrative buildings.

After a hotly contested referendum on Crimea's status, Russia quickly annexed the area. With significant but covert support from Russia, pro-Russian rebels in eastern Ukraine's Donbas region announced the Donetsk People's Republic and the Luhansk People's Republic in April 2014. Late in 2014, Ukrainian attempts to reclaim territories held by separatists failed, sparking a lengthy conflict in the Donbas. Despite its continuous denials, Russian troops actively took part in the unreported conflict. The Minsk II agreements, which were signed in an effort to put an end to the conflict in February 2015 by both Russia and Ukraine, were never fully carried out. The fighting in Donbas between Ukraine and Russian proxies became brutal but static, with intermittent brief ceasefires but no enduring calm and few shifts in control of territory.

Russia started to amass a sizable military presence close to its border with Ukraine in 2021, including from inside Belarus' neighbor. Vladimir Putin, the president of Russia, opposed NATO's expansion and asked that Ukraine be prevented from ever joining the military alliance. Additionally, he aired revanchist opinions and questioned Ukraine's legitimacy to exist. Russia formally acknowledged the independence of the Donetsk and Luhansk People's Republics on February 21, 2022. A full-scale invasion of Ukraine began three days later when Putin declared a "special military operation" there in a television broadcast. International condemnation of the invasion prompted many nations to start imposing sanctions against Russia and tighten those that already existed. In the face of ferocious resistance, Russia abandoned an attempt to seize Kiev in early April 2022.

Since August, Ukrainian counteroffensives in the south and northeast have recaptured considerable territory. Russia announced the annexation of a number of southern and eastern Ukrainian regions towards the end of September, despite the fact that its forces were not yet completely occupying those areas. This announcement sparked strong criticism from many quarters. Tens of thousands of people have died as a result of the ongoing civil war, which has also caused a significant refugee crisis.

Inflation will increase and supply chain pressures will worsen as the war between Russia and Ukraine intensifies in the wake of Russia's full-scale invasion at the end of February. As the situation worsens, there may be more market volatility as investors seek out safe havens and some transactions are delayed. While the military operations are still ongoing, geopolitical and economic unpredictability are expected to remain high. The Organization for Economic Cooperation and Development said Monday that the invasion of Ukraine by Russia will cost the world economy $2.8 trillion in lost output by the end of the year, and considerably more if a harsh winter causes energy restrictions in Europe.

1.6 The Armed Racing

In 2021, global military spending increased further and surpassed $2.1 trillion for the first time on developing, exporting, and using military personnel and equipment results in yearly expenditures to countries of hundreds of billions of dollars. World military spending reached the historic levels, notwithstanding the economic effects of the Covid-19 outbreak, according to Dr. Diego Lopes da Silva, Senior Researcher with SIPRI's Military Expenditure and Arms Production Programme. "Inflation caused a slowdown in the rate of real-terms growth."

US military expenditures totaled $801 billion in 2021, a 1.4% decrease from 2020. The cost of the US military declined marginally from 3.7% of GDP in 2020 to 3.5% in 2021. Between 2012 and 2021, US funding for military research and development (R&D) increased by 24%, while funding for arms purchase decreased by 6.4%. Spending on both fell in 2021. Nevertheless, the decline in R&D spending (-1.2%) was less severe than the decline in arms purchase spending (−5.4 per cent). The rise in R&D expenditure for the period 2012–21 implies that the United States is placing more emphasis on next-generation technology, the Military Expenditure and Arms Production Programme researcher Alexandra Marksteiner said. The US Government has emphasized the need of maintaining the US military's technological advantage over strategic rivals on numerous occasions.

In terms of military spending, the United States was the top country in 2021, spending $801 billion, or over 38% of all military spending worldwide. Since SIPRI started keeping track in 1949, America has been the nation with the highest military expenditures, accounting for more than 30% of global military spending during the past 20 years. The United States spent more on its military in 2021 than all other countries in the top 10 combined, a rise of $22.3 billion year over year.

China came in second place in terms of military spending in 2021, spending $293.4 billion, or approximately 14% of all military expenditures worldwide. China has grown its military spending for 27 years in a row, despite the fact that its budget is still less than half that of the United States. China really has the most active military personnel overall, and its military spending has increased significantly over the past ten years.

Russian military budget, which totaled $65.9 billion in 2021, placed it only sixth among all countries, but as a percentage of GDP, it ranked among the higher-ranking countries. Saudi Arabia, which spent 6.6% of its GDP on the military, was the only country in the top 10 to spend more than

Russia (4.1% of GDP). Seismic geopolitical changes brought forth by Russia's invasion of Ukraine in February have sparked a wave of international weapons exports and international cooperation. Since the start of the crisis, the U.S. has provided $8.2 billion in security aid to Ukraine, demonstrating how allies may help offset some of the cost of domestic military spending.

In a similar manner, China and Russia have strengthened their ties, exchanging military technology and intelligence and starting joint military exercises at the end of August with other countries like India, Belarus, Mongolia, and Tajikistan. Putin mentioned Russia's preparedness to export weaponry as being "years, or maybe even decades ahead of their international counterparts" when he mentioned China's achievement in hypersonic missile flight a year ago. Russia has since started testing its own versions of the technology.

Chapter II. Global and Regional Organizations

This chapter explores the development of regional organizations in Asia and the world, specifically in East and Southeast Asia, as well as their interactions with international organizations on a larger scale. Background for this analysis will be provided by a variety of topics that relate to both the long-standing difficulties of regional cooperation and the more recent ramifications of the altering global balance of power. Asia has long struggled to create regional organizations and procedures for addressing common problems. The region has been characterized by bilateral partnerships and informal alliances, and cooperation has been hindered by the region's history of protracted armed war and its legacy, as well as by ongoing political disputes between important states. Institutionalized regional cooperation has been hampered by the Westphalian political culture of the area, which emphasizes state sovereignty, territorial integrity, and non-interference.

Asia's participation in regional and international organizations has been a reflection of the recent changes to the international landscape. With regard to economic growth, there has been a global shift in attention toward Asia, and this has led to increasing success on a regional level. The politics of regional organizations and, to a lesser extent, Asia's participation in international organizations reflect the dynamics of the post-Cold War world order, particularly the "rising" of non-Western nations. As a result, Asia has resisted "Westernized" institutions and norms, developed substitute multilateral agreements, and produced conflict over the standards of global society and authority over the international agenda. In light of the shifting nature of the international order, there are additional concerns about the US's continued presence in Asia, particularly with regard to its connections with important allies like South Korea and Japan and its rivalry with China.

The key political tendencies of the region are thus raised by a study of Asia's regional and international organizations. Will the shift in the global economy toward Asia create new motivations for regionalism, overcoming earlier barriers to tighter cooperation? Will the dynamics of Asia's regional cooperation and its engagement with international organizations be impacted by the global transfer in power, in which Asia is a driving force? Will Asia support normative adjustments in terms of the values that guide regional and international organizations? What are the ramifications of a potential US hegemonic fall; will it lead to longer-term regional collaboration or destabilization and conflict? What kind of leadership might emerging nations—especially China—display in the future development of Asia's regional order?

2.1 The United Nation

The United Nations (UN) is an intergovernmental body whose declared goals are to uphold world peace and security, foster goodwill among nations, promote global collaboration, and serve as a hub for harmonizing national policies. It is the biggest and best-known international organization in the world. The UN has main offices in Geneva, Nairobi, Vienna, and The Hague in addition to its worldwide headquarters in New York City (home to the International Court of Justice).

The League of Nations was replaced by the UN in order to avert future world wars after World War II because it was deemed inefficient. 50 nations gathered in San Francisco on April 25, 1945, for a conference, and began drafting the UN Charter, which was approved on June 25, 1945, and went into effect on October 24, 1945, when the UN officially commenced operations. The organization's goals are listed in the Charter and include preserving world peace and security, defending human rights, providing humanitarian help, fostering sustainable development, and upholding international law. With the accession of South Sudan in 2011, the UN's membership has increased from 51 to 193, nearly all of the world's sovereign governments being represented.

The Cold War between the United States and the Soviet Union and their respective allies hindered the organization's early efforts to maintain world peace. Its missions have mostly involved lightly armed personnel and unarmed military observers who perform monitoring, reporting, and confidence-building tasks. After substantial decolonization began in the 1960s, the number of UN members increased significantly. Since that time, 80 former colonies—among them 11 trust areas that the Trusteeship Council had been charged with overseeing—have been independent. By the 1970s, the UN was spending significantly more on economic and social development initiatives than on maintaining peace. The UN changed and extended its field activities after the Cold War ended, taking on a wide range of difficult responsibilities.

The General Assembly, Security Council, Economic and Social Council (ECOSOC), Trusteeship Council, International Court of Justice, and UN Secretariat are the six main bodies that make up the UN. Numerous specialized organizations, programs, and initiatives are part of the UN System, including the World Bank Group, the World Health Organization, the World Food Program, UNESCO, and UNICEF. In order to engage in the activities of the UN, non-governmental groups may also be granted consultative status with ECOSOC and other organizations. The secretary-general of the UN, who is now the politician and diplomat from Portugal named António Guterres, began his first five-year term on January 1 of this year and was re-elected on June 8, 2021. The group is supported through assessed and free donations from its member states.

Despite varied reviews of its efficacy, the UN, its officials, and its agencies have received numerous Nobel Peace Prizes. While some observers have criticized the organization as ineffectual, biased, or corrupt, others see it as a powerful force for world peace and human progress. In order to uphold the provisions of peace agreements and deter combatants from resuming hostilities, the UN dispatches peacekeepers to areas where armed conflict has just ended or paused after receiving approval from the Security Council. Member states voluntarily send peacekeeping personnel because the UN does not have its own military. Because of their striking uniforms, these soldiers are commonly referred to as "Blue Helmets." The Nobel Peace Prize was given to peacekeeping organizations as a whole in 1988.

The UN has also come under fire for alleged shortcomings. Member nations have frequently showed unwillingness to implement or uphold Security Council resolutions. Conflicts in the Security Council over military intervention and action are believed to have prevented the genocides in Cambodia in the 1970s, Rwanda in 1994, and Bangladesh in 1971. Similar to how UN inaction is held accountable for not ending the Somali Civil War peacekeeping operations in 1992–93 or stopping the 1995 Srebrenica slaughter. Additionally, throughout numerous peacekeeping operations in the Democratic Republic of the Congo, Haiti, Liberia, Sudan and what is now South Sudan, Burundi, and Côte d'Ivoire, UN forces have been charged with child rape, soliciting prostitutes, and sexual abuse. As the most likely cause of the 2010s Haiti cholera outbreak, which claimed more than 8,000 lives after the 2010 Haiti earthquake, scientists pointed to UN peacekeepers from Nepal.

The UN actively promotes disarmament in addition to maintaining peace. When the UN Charter was being drafted in 1945, regulation of arms was considered a measure to restrict the use of financial and human resources in their production. Only a few weeks after the charter was signed, nuclear weapons were developed, prompting the first General Assembly resolution to ask for detailed suggestions for "the elimination of atomic weapons and of all other major weapons of mass destruction from national arsenal." The UN has participated in arms-limitation treaties like the Ottawa Treaty (1997), which outlaws landmines, the Outer Space Treaty (1967), the Treaty on the Non-Proliferation of Nuclear Weapons (1968), the Seabed Arms Control Treaty (1971), the Biological Weapons Convention (1972), the Chemical Weapons Convention (1992), and the Seabed Arms Control Treaty (1997).

The International Atomic Energy Agency, the Organization for the Prohibition of Chemical Weapons, and the Comprehensive Nuclear-Test-Ban Treaty Organization Preparatory Commission are the three UN agencies in charge of overseeing matters related to arms proliferation. Furthermore, disarmament is a major component of many peacekeeping missions. For example, operations in West Africa disarmed about 250,000 former combatants and secured tens of thousands of guns and millions of rounds of ammunition.

2.2 World Trade Organization

An intergovernmental body that controls and promotes global trade is the World Trade Organization (WTO). Governments use the United Nations System with effective cooperation to create, update, and enforce the laws that regulate international trade. According to the 1994 Marrakesh Agreement, it began operating formally on January 1st, 1995, taking the place of the 1948-established General Agreement on Tariffs and Trade (GATT). The WTO, which has 164 members and represents more than 98% of world commerce and GDP, is the largest international economic organization in the world.

The WTO provides a framework for trade agreements that typically seek to decrease or remove tariffs, quotas, and other limitations. These agreements are signed by representatives of member states and confirmed by their legislatures. The WTO enables trade in products, services, and intellectual property between participating countries. In order to ensure that parties follow trade agreements and settle issues pertaining to trade, the WTO also oversees impartial dispute settlement. Although the organization forbids discrimination between trading partners, it makes exceptions for critical objectives including national security and environmental protection.

The headquarters of the WTO are in Geneva, Switzerland. The Ministerial Conference, which consists of all of its member nations and typically meets every two years, is its primary decision-making body, and all decisions are made with a focus on agreement. The General Council, which is made up of representatives from all members, is in charge of daily operations. Over 600 employees make up the Secretariat, which is overseen by the Director-General and his four deputies and offers administrative, professional, and technical services. The WTO's annual budget is around 220 million USD, and countries contribute according to their share of global trade.

According to studies, the WTO has increased commerce and lowered trade barriers. It has also had an impact on trade agreements more broadly; according to a 2017 research, the great majority of preferential trade agreements (PTAs) that had been signed up to that time expressly referred to the WTO and contained large amounts of material that was lifted from WTO accords. The WTO accords were mentioned in UN Sustainable Development Goal 10 as tools for addressing inequality. However, some claim that the advantages of free trade that the WTO facilitates are not distributed fairly.

Additionally, it is the responsibility of the WTO to examine, promote, and ensure the coherence and transparency of national trade policies through oversight of the formulation of global economic policy. Assistance for developing, least-developed, and low-income countries in transition to adapt to WTO rules and disciplines through technical cooperation and training is another objective of the WTO.

1. The WTO shall provide the framework for the multilateral trade agreements' implementation, administration, and operation as well as facilitate their implementation,

operation, and advancement of the purposes of this Agreement and the multilateral trade agreements.

2. In topics covered by the Agreement in the Annexes to this Agreement, the WTO shall act as the platform for negotiations among its members about their multilateral trade relations.

3. The Understanding on Rules and Procedures Governing the Settlement of Disputes shall be administered by the WTO.

4. A Trade Policy Review Mechanism will be managed by the WTO.

5. The WTO should collaborate, as appropriate, with the International Monetary Fund (IMF), the International Bank for Reconstruction and Development (IBRD), and its affiliated organizations to increase coherence in the formulation of international economic policy.

The World Trade Organization also performs the five tasks listed above. An international organization is required to oversee the trading systems as globalization continues to advance in today's society. Due to the variations in each country's trading regulations, problems including protectionism, trade barriers, subsidies, and intellectual property violations occur when the volume of commerce rises. When such issues emerge, the World Trade Organization acts as a mediator between the governments. One of the most significant institutions in the modern globalized world and the product of globalization is the WTO.

The WTO is also a hub for economic research and analysis; it regularly evaluates the state of world trade in its annual publications and publishes research studies on certain subjects. The WTO also works closely with the IMF and the World Bank, the other two Bretton Woods system elements.

According to studies, the WTO increased trade. According to research, the average country would see a 32 percentage point increase in export tariffs in the absence of the WTO. One strategy to increase trade is through the WTO's dispute resolution process.

A 2017 study published in the Journal of International Economic Law found that "almost all contemporary preferential trade agreements (PTAs) expressly refer to the WTO, frequently many times over the course of many chapters. The WTO has been more prevalent in PTAs over time, as seen by the considerable amounts of treaty language—and perhaps the bulk of a chapter—that are taken directly from WTO agreements.

2.3 The Shanghai Cooperation Organization

An intergovernmental body called the Shanghai Cooperation Organization (SCO) was established on June 15, 2001, in Shanghai. Currently, the SCO consists of eight Member States (China, India, Kazakhstan, Kyrgyzstan, Russia, Pakistan, Tajikistan, and Uzbekistan), four Observer States (Afghanistan, Belarus, Iran, and Mongolia) that are interested in obtaining full membership, and six "Dialogue Partners" (Armenia, Azerbaijan, Cambodia, Nepal, Sri Lanka and Turkey). In 2021, it was decided to begin the process of Iran becoming a full member of the SCO, and Egypt, Qatar, and Saudi Arabia were made conversation partners.

The Shanghai Cooperation Organization (SCO) is a political, economic, international security, and defense organization based in Eurasia. It is the largest regional organization in the world in terms of both population and geographic coverage, accounting for more than 30% of the world's GDP and over 60% of Eurasia.

A permanent intergovernmental international organization, the Shanghai Cooperation Organization was established on June 15, 2001 in Shanghai by six nations: the People's Republic of China, the Russian Federation, the Republics of Kazakhstan, Kyrgyzstan, Tajikistan, and Uzbekistan. The "Shanghai Five" method served as the foundation for its establishment.

The Shanghai Cooperation Organization's main goals are to promote effective cooperation among its member states in political, economic, trade, scientific, technological, cultural, and educational spheres as well as in the fields of energy, transportation, tourism, and environmental protection; to jointly safeguard and present regional peace, security, and stability; and to work towards the creation of democratic, just, and peaceful societies.

The SCO's internal interactions are governed by "the Spirit of Shanghai," which is founded on the values of equality, mutual benefit, mutual trust, respect for many cultures, and a desire for collaborative progress. External ties are governed by the same principles. SCO does not target any particular governments or areas and is not a closed block.

The highest decision-making body is the Council of Heads of Member States. It meets regularly once a year and decides and gives directions on all significant issues facing the Organization. Once a year, the Council of Heads of Governments of SCO Member States meets regularly to discuss multilateral cooperation strategy and priority directions within the framework of the organization, to decide on actual matters of principle pertaining to economic and other cooperation, and to approve the organization's budget for the following year. Along with the annual gatherings of the Councils of Heads of State and Government, there are also meetings of the Ministers of Foreign Affairs, the Ministers of the Economy, Transport, Culture, Defense, and Security, the General Public Prosecutors, the Heads of the Border, and the Ministry of Extreme Measures authorities. Within the SCO framework, the Council of National Coordinators of SCO Member States acts as the coordination mechanism.

The Secretariat in Beijing and the Regional Anti-Terrorist Structure (RATS) in Tashkent are the two permanent organizations that make up the Shanghai Cooperation Organization. The Council of Heads of State appoints the Secretary-General and the Director of the Executive Committee for three years. A quarter of the world's population, or 1.455 billion people, live in the SCO member nations, which collectively occupy an area of around 30 million 189 thousand square kilometers, or almost three fifths of Eurasia.

The Roles of Shanghai Cooperation Organization

The Shanghai Cooperation Organization (SCO) was founded as a multinational organization to promote trade, cultural exchange, and humanitarian cooperation. Its goals include ensuring security and maintaining stability throughout the large Eurasian region. The SCO seeks to create a just polycentric world order that is fully compliant with international law norms and mutual respect principles, which serves the interests of each and every State while taking into account their shared needs and aspirations. This is done by fostering mutually beneficial cooperation, averting conflict and confrontation, and maintaining equal and indivisible security. The SCO works to prevent the clash of civilizations among its many regions as a global organization with a diverse membership.

SCO does not anticipate joining any alliances or direct its actions against any sovereign state in accordance with the openness principles. It purposefully and steadfastly pursues communication, exchanges, and cooperation and upholds the strict observance of the goals and values outlined in the United Nations Charter, including respect for the territorial integrity and inviolability of borders, non-aggression, peaceful dispute resolution, and refraining from using or threatening to use force against other nations or people.

The organization's overall structure is intended to foster multilateral collaborations that will help sovereign members coordinate their plans and tactics for resolving urgent global problems and addressing local needs. Additionally, it gives member states the chance to focus their efforts on shared objectives in accordance with the concepts of unforced collaboration and equal responsibility distribution.

A new phase in the growth of the organization began with the historic SCO heads of state summit held in Astana, Kazakhstan, on June 8 and 9, 2017. The admission of India and Pakistan to the SCO as full members was one of its main outcomes. The SCO has been able to increase its capacity and broaden its range of options, notably in the area of fending off present and potential dangers and challenges, thanks to the accession of these two strong and significant South Asian nations.

With nearly 44% of the world's population living in the SCO member states' vast region, which stretches from the Arctic to the Indian Ocean and from Lianyungang in China to Kaliningrad in the Russian Federation, the responsibility of what is currently the world's largest regional organization is to maintain stability and effectively combat security threats across our respective territories. The Strategic Cooperation Organization (SCO), which unites four nuclear powers—or half of the nuclear States in the world—into a single regional organization, acts as an additional deterrent within the framework designed to preserve the strategic balance of power and political stability throughout the world.

The Astana Declaration of the Heads of State of the Shanghai Cooperation Organization, which is a result document of the Astana summit, also outlines additional steps the organization will take against threats to global peace and security in addition to agreements reached by SCO member states on important issues on the regional and global agendas. Methods and Realistic Measures for Security and Stability

SCO is unwavering in its conviction that diplomacy is the best method for resolving disputes, adhering to the strict adherence of generally accepted norms of international law and the unrelenting pursuit of the goals and objectives of the United Nations Charter. In this regard, the SCO maintains its support for the UN playing an even larger coordination role in international affairs, with a focus on the growth of close collaboration with the global Organization.

A number of special projects created under the aegis of the United Nations and SCO have significantly improved global collaboration in addressing shared security threats and concerns. The results of the High-Level Special Event on "The United Nations and the Shanghai Cooperation Organization: Jointly Countering Challenges and Threats," hosted in November 2016 in New York, and the high-level side event on "The United Nations and Shanghai Cooperation Organization in the Fight Against Drugs: Common Threats and Joint Actions," held in March 2017 in Vienna in partnership with the United Nations Office on Drugs and Crime, serve as examples.

Expanding dialogue and strengthening collaboration in order to ensure comprehensive security by combating terrorism, cyberterrorism, separatism, extremism, transnational organized crime, and illicit drug trafficking, as well as strengthening global information security and emergency response, is what SCO will continue to do.

Regarding this, the SCO plans to advance the Regional Anti-Terrorist Structure, which is the organization's main permanent entity (RATS). The magnitude of RATS's effectiveness in its efforts is plainly demonstrated by the data. Averting 650 acts of a terrorist and extremist nature, neutralizing 440 terrorist training camps, and eliminating 1,700 members of international terrorist organizations were all accomplished between 2011 and 2015 by the authorities of SCO member States working in conjunction with RATS.

More than 2,700 illegal armed group members, their allies, and individuals suspected of engaging in criminal activity were detained, while 213 individuals linked to terrorist or extremist groups were extradited and many received lengthy prison sentences; 180 suspects were added to wanted lists; 600 undercover bases housing weapons were exposed; more than 3,250 improvised explosive devices, 10,000 weapons, roughly 450,000 pieces.

The SCO Declaration on Countering Extremism, which was approved during the summit in Astana, is the organization's joint reaction to the constantly expanding menace of extremism. Along with the Shanghai Convention on Combating Terrorism, Separatism, and Extremism, the Convention of the Shanghai Cooperation Organization against Terrorism, the 2016-2018

SCO Member States Program on Cooperation in Combating Terrorism, Separatism, and Extremism, and core United Nations instruments like the United Nations Global Counter-Terrorism Strategy, this document will strengthen the international legal framework for countering emerging challenges and threats. The SCO Convention on Countering Extremism aims to improve the legal environment in this area while also strengthening security and enhancing effective cooperation amongst agencies.

An increase in terrorist operations across the globe necessitates the creation and advancement of current methods and strategies used in our shared struggle against this evil. The Statement by the Heads of the Member States of the SCO on Joint Counteraction to International Terrorism issued in Astana is a significant political document that contains an evaluation of the situation, strategies for bolstering our joint forces in the war against terrorism, and a call to action for the international community to come together as part of a broad-based international anti-terrorist coalition to combat this grave global threat.

Under the circumstances, it has been especially risky for extremist ideology and propaganda to proliferate, including the public justification of terrorism as a method of inciting others to perform terrorist attacks. In this context, the SCO will intensify cooperative initiatives to combat societal radicalization, which gives rise to the worst manifestations of extremism, including terrorism, particularly among young people. Additionally, we are taking action to combat xenophobia, ethnic and racial intolerance, and political, religious, and ethnic extremism.

The potential for voluntary and responsible contributions from civil society, including traditional religious organizations, educational and research institutions, mass media, and non-governmental organizations operating in SCO member States in accordance with international law, will also receive special attention in addition to cooperation between law enforcement authorities and judicial bodies.

Following the guidelines of the 2015 Agreement on Cooperation and Interaction of the SCO Member States on Border Issues and the 2006 Agreement on Cooperation in Identifying and Blocking the Channels of Penetration on the

Territory of the SCO Member States of Individuals Involved in Terrorist, Separatist, and Extremist Activities, member States will continue their cooperation in preventing malicious activities and movement of foreign terrorists, militants, and terrorists.

Members of the SCO will work together to combat any attempts by people or groups to recruit, train, and use terrorists, to spread terrorist propaganda, or to justify or finance terrorist attacks.

Despite the fact that the SCO is not a military alliance, our frontline defense against terrorist threats necessitates that we continue to refine and improve the systems designed to completely eradicate terrorist activity. The SCO Peace Mission exercise is one of the scheduled anti-terrorist training exercises that will continue in this regard. Building on the Agreement on Cooperation in Ensuring International Digital Security amongst SCO Member States, we will also intensify our cooperation in combating radical propaganda and public justification of terrorism, separatism, and extremism in mass media and the information sphere.

One of SCO's fundamental priorities is to stop the trafficking of illegal drugs

The manufacture and trafficking of illegal drugs continue to pose one of the biggest security risks to global peace and stability. In accordance with the provisions of United Nations conventions and resolutions, including the conclusions of the Special Session of the United Nations General Assembly on the World Drug Problem, held in April 2016 in New York, SCO will further develop its 2004 Agreement on Cooperation between SCO Member States in Combating Illicit Trafficking of Drugs, Psychotropic Substances, and Precursors, 2015 Statement by the Heads of SCO Member States on Drug Threat.

69 tons of lethal heroin were taken from traffickers during special anti-drug operations carried out within SCO borders over the previous five years, demonstrating the success of our combined efforts in this sector. This amount represents about 14% of the drugs that have been seized worldwide. The illegal synthesis of narcotic poisons required 75 tons of precursors, which were discovered thanks to effective law enforcement cooperation. Authorities from SCO member states' cooperation

turned out to be largely successful. However, the entire international community's actions will need to be combined in order to effectively battle the drug problem. In this regard, the SCO plans to keep up its close working relationship with the UN Office on Drugs and Crime.

Economic Growth as Tool for Preventing the Development of New Security Challenges and Threats

Uneven economic development around the globe causes extremism and, ultimately, potentially fatal war scenarios. Negative trends in the growth of the world economy exacerbate existing imbalances, which in turn fuel an increase in the dangers and difficulties facing security and sustainable development. In light of this, SCO stands for extensive international collaboration in fostering global economic recovery, guaranteeing financial and economic stability, and sustaining sustainable, dynamic, balanced, and inclusive growth in a setting that is fast becoming more global. Members of the SCO concur that the principles of transparency, non-discrimination, and the rejection of protectionist tactics must be followed in the conduct of global commerce.

Trade must be founded on laws that are equitably applied to all parties. In order to encourage the development of an open global economy that will support the multilateral trading system, it is crucial to remove current trade barriers and stop the establishment of new ones. SCO will take extra steps to assist the growth of regional economies, create favorable trade conditions, encourage investment initiatives, improve infrastructure, create industrial parks where the right circumstances allow, and increase the standard of living for the local populations.

The implementation of the SCO Member States' Agreement on Creating Favorable Conditions for International Road Transportation, which was signed in Dushanbe, Tajikistan, in September 2014, is a significant practical step in that direction. The treaty-based foundation for the multilateral comprehensive development of regional infrastructure and an integrated system of road transportation, this agreement not only establishes equitable conditions for managing the trade flow from Eastern Europe to the Russian east coast and China for the benefit of both parties.

As a Preventive Measure against Security Threats, Cultural Dialogue

Collaboration in the fields of culture, education, and science is crucial to building mutual trust, friendliness, and good neighborly ties amongst SCO member states. A strong foundation for ongoing cultural exchanges among SCO members promotes mutual understanding by educating each other about and enhancing one another's cultural experiences. In order to combat xenophobia, religious intolerance, and prejudice based on ethnic and racial background, cultural discourse brings people together and unites them around shared humanistic values and ambitions. The SCO's fundamental objective of bringing civilizations together is included in this debate.

Cultural sites that make up 20% of the UNESCO World Heritage List at the moment are tangible examples of the rich historical and cultural legacies of the peoples of the SCO countries. Understanding these sites offers a rare chance to get to know the rich history of the Eurasian region, take in the variety of its distinctive national and cultural characteristics, and have a greater sense of the mindset and worldview of its residents.

Our efforts to advance peace, ensure security, and advance sustainable development will continue to place a high priority on enhancing cultural interactions within the SCO region, enhancing mutual understanding among its peoples, respecting their cultural traditions and customs, and preserving and enhancing cultural diversity within SCO member States. These important objectives can be accomplished through planning international exhibitions, festivals, and contests, fostering cross-national cooperation, and continuing scholarly investigations into the region's cultural and natural heritage.

2.4 The NATO

With 30 members—28 European and 2 North American—the North Atlantic Treaty Organization (NATO), commonly known as the North Atlantic Alliance, is an intergovernmental military alliance. The North Atlantic Treaty was put into effect by the organization after World War II, with its signing in Washington, D.C., on April 4, 1949. The independent member states of NATO have agreed to defend one another from outside attacks as a form of collective security. NATO functioned as a check on the imagined Soviet Union threat during the Cold War. After the fall of the Soviet Union, the alliance persisted and has participated in military actions in South Asia, Africa, the Middle East, and the Balkans.

NATO's central command are close to the Belgian town of Mons, while the organization's main offices are in Brussels. The combined military of all NATO nations number about 3.5 million soldiers and personnel, and the organization has focused its NATO Response Force deployments in Eastern Europe. By 2020, their combined military expenditures made up more than 57 percent of the nominal world total. Members also agreed to meet or maintain the aim of at least 2% of GDP for defense spending by 2024.

In the wake of World War II and at the outset of the Cold War, France and the United Kingdom signed the Treaty of Dunkirk on March 4, 1947, as a treaty of alliance and mutual assistance in the case of potential attacks by Germany or the Soviet Union. The Benelux nations were added to this alliance in March 1948 as part of the Treaty of Brussels, creating the Brussels Treaty Organization, also known as the Western Union.

The Truman Doctrine, the country's foreign policy, encouraged international solidarity against what it saw as communist aggression, such as the February 1948 coup d'état in Czechoslovakia. Talks for a larger military alliance, which could include North America, also started that month in the United States. The Western Union members, along with the United States, Canada, Portugal, Italy, Norway, Denmark, and Iceland, signed the North Atlantic Treaty on April 4, 1949, as a result of these negotiations. Lester B. Pearson, a diplomat from Canada, was a main creator and drafter of the pact.

Prior to the Korean War, the North Atlantic Treaty was mostly dormant, and NATO's founding was what allowed it to be put into effect with an integrated military structure. This included the establishment of Supreme Headquarters Allied Powers Europe (SHAPE) in 1951, which took over much of the military institutions and strategies of the Western Union, including their agreements on equipment standardization and the stationing of foreign military forces in European nations. The position of NATO Secretary General was created as the group's top civilian position in 1952.

In addition, Greece and Turkey joined the alliance that year, and Exercise Mainbrace, one of the first significant NATO naval exercises, took place. West Germany was given permission to rearmament after the London and Paris Conferences, and as a result, they joined NATO in May 1955. This, in turn, had a significant role in the formation of the Warsaw Pact, which was dominated by the Soviet Union and defined the two sides of the Cold War.

When the Berlin Wall was constructed in 1961, there were 400,000 US troops stationed in Europe, and tensions were at their highest. Questions about the strength of the alliance between the European nations and the United States fluctuated, as did doubts about the NATO defense against a potential Soviet invasion. These doubts prompted France to create its own nuclear deterrent and leave NATO's military structure in 1966. Spain, which had just gained democracy, joined the coalition in 1982.

The 1989 European Revolutions prompted a strategic reevaluation of NATO's goals, missions, and regional focus. East Germany joined the alliance and the Federal Republic of Germany in October 1990, and the alliance and the Soviet Union signed the Treaty on Conventional Armed Forces in Europe (CFE) in Paris in November 1990. It required particular military cuts across the continent, which persisted after the Soviet Union's breakup in December 1991 and the Warsaw Pact's collapse in February 1991, which eliminated the de facto principal NATO foes.

This marked the start of a decrease in military funding and supplies in Europe. In the subsequent sixteen years, the CFE treaty's signatories were able to destroy 52,000 conventional weapons, which reduced military spending by NATO's European countries by 28% from 1990 to 2015. According to notes of secret meetings, various Western leaders assured Mikhail Gorbachev in 1990 that NATO would not move further east. However, the subject of eastward expansion was not addressed in the final wording of the Treaty on the Final

Settlement with Respect to Germany, which was signed later that year.

The organization expanded its operations into political and humanitarian issues that had not previously been of concern to NATO in the 1990s. The group launched its initial military operations in Bosnia from 1992 to 1995, and then in Yugoslavia in 1999, after the breakup of Yugoslavia. These wars served as the impetus for a significant post-Cold War military rebuilding. The Headquarters Allied Command Europe Rapid Reaction Corps and other new units were developed after NATO's military organization was reduced and rebuilt.

During this post-Cold War era, diplomatic forums for regional cooperation between NATO and its neighbors were established, including the Partnership for Peace and the Mediterranean Dialogue initiative in 1994, the Euro-Atlantic Partnership Council in 1997, and the NATO-Russia Permanent Joint Council in 1998. Politically, the organization sought better relations with the newly autonomous Central and Eastern European states. At the 1999 Washington summit, NATO officially admitted Hungary, Poland, and the Czech Republic.

The alliance also released new membership requirements with unique "Membership Action Plans."

As a result of these initiatives, the following nations have joined the alliance: Montenegro in 2017, North Macedonia in 2020, Albania and Croatia in 2009, Bulgaria, Estonia, Latvia, Lithuania, Romania, Slovakia, and Slovenia in 2004. After Nicolas Sarkozy was elected as the country's president in 2007, France underwent a significant military reform that culminated on 4 April 2009 with the country's return to full membership, which also saw France re-join the NATO Military Command Structure while retaining its own nuclear deterrent.

After the September 11 attacks, the North Atlantic Treaty's Article 5, which mandates that members defend any member state under armed attack, was used for the first and only time, leading to the deployment of soldiers to Afghanistan under the command of the NATO-led ISAF. Since then, the group has performed a number of additional tasks, including as sending trainers to Iraq, helping with anti-piracy activities, and in 2011, imposing a no-fly zone over Libya in compliance with UN Security Council Resolution 1973.

One of the seven occasions when Article 4, which requires consultation among NATO members, has been used was in response to Russia's annexation of Crimea. In the past, there was the Iraq War and the Syrian Civil War. The leaders of NATO member states publicly pledged to spend at least two percent of their gross domestic products on defense by 2024 at the Wales summit in 2014, which had previously merely been an informal guideline. The construction of the NATO Enhanced Forward Presence, which sent four multinational battalion-sized battle groups to Estonia, Latvia, Lithuania, and Poland, was approved by NATO members at the 2016 Warsaw summit.

Several NATO nations sent ground forces, warships, and fighter planes to bolster the alliance's eastern flank before and during the Russian invasion of Ukraine in 2022, and numerous nations once more referred to Article 4. NATO leaders gathered in Brussels for an unusual summit in March 2022 that also included leaders from the Group of Seven and the European Union. Four further battlegroups will be established by NATO member states in Bulgaria, Hungary, Romania, and Slovakia.

Additionally, the NATO Response Force's first-ever elements have been activated.

To thwart Russian assault, NATO had stationed 40,000 troops along its 2,500-kilometer Eastern flank as of June 2022. With a combined ex-NATO force of 259,000 soldiers, the five countries of Bulgaria, Romania, Hungary, Slovakia, and Poland have deployed more than half of this total. Spain contributed Eurofighter Typhoons, the Netherlands sent eight F-35s, and more French and US attack planes would soon be arriving to supplement Bulgaria's Air Force. All of its member states' citizens support NATO.

2.5 The BRICS

The name BRICS stands for Brazil, Russia, India, China, and South Africa, five of the world's largest rising economies. Jim O'Neill, an economist at Goldman Sachs, first referred to the first four as "BRIC" in 2001. O'Neill used the phrase to indicate rapidly expanding economies that would collectively control the world economy by 2050; South Africa was included in 2010.

With a combined territory of 39,746,220 km2 (15,346,100 sq mi) and a projected population of around 3.21 billion, the BRICS account for about 26.7% of the planet's land area and 41.5% of its people. By population, area, and GDP, Brazil, Russia, India, and China are among the top ten most populous, largest, and richest nations in the world. The last three are also usually regarded as existing or upcoming superpowers.

All five countries are G20 members, with a combined nominal GDP of US$26.6 trillion (about 26.2% of the global GDP), a total GDP (PPP) of US$51.99 trillion (roughly 32.1% of the global GDP PPP), and estimated combined foreign reserves of US$4.46 trillion. The BRICS were not a recognized intergovernmental body when they were first identified; rather, they were used to advertise investment opportunities. Their governments meet formally each year at summits to coordinate multilateral policy, and since 2009, they have become a more coherent geopolitical bloc. On July 24, 2022, China held the most recent BRICS summit. The primary tenets of bilateral ties between the BRICS countries are non-interference, equality, and mutual interest.

By proposing competing efforts like the New Development Bank, Contingent Reserve Arrangement, BRICS payment system, and BRICS basket reserve currency, the BRICS are seen as the G7 club of leading rich economies' main adversaries. The association has been working to grow its membership since 2022, and several developing nations have expressed an interest in joining. There have been many analysts who have praised and criticized the BRICS.

Argentina and Iran are just two of the many nations that have indicated interest in joining the BRIC grouping (also known as BRICS) since South Africa did so in 2010. During talks with senior Chinese officials, the current BRICS chair, throughout the course of the summer of 2022, both expressed their determination to join BRICS. Following a meeting between Chinese State Councilor and Foreign Minister Wang Yi and Argentine Foreign Minister Santiago Cafiero on the sidelines of the G20 Summit in Indonesia, Beijing supported Argentina's potential membership.

When Cafiero and Yi later met on the sidelines of the 77th UN General Assembly, China once more reaffirmed their support for Argentina's probable application. It is also acknowledged that Brazil, Russia, and India support Argentina's application. Iran also applied to join the Chinese government's economic association of emerging markets in June 2022. In recent months, relations between Iran, China, and Russia have improved as all three regimes look for new partners to counter growing Western criticism. While they have not yet made official requests, Saudi Arabia, Turkey, and Egypt have also shown an interest in joining the BRICS. Although there isn't a formal application procedure per se to join BRICS, any prospective member state must gain the support of all current BRICS members—Brazil, Russia, India, China, and South Africa—in order to be sent an invitation.

BRICS's Developments

The BRICS Forum was established in 2011 as an independent international group promoting collaboration in business, politics, and culture between the BRICS countries. The BRICS nations offered $75 billion in June 2012 to increase the International Monetary Fund's capacity to lend (IMF). This loan, however, was subject to IMF voting reforms. The member nations of the fifth BRICS summit in Durban, South Africa, at the end of March 2013, decided to establish a global financial organization to work alongside the western-dominated IMF and World Bank. Following the summit, the BRICS announced their intention to complete the plans for this New Development Bank by 2014. However, disagreements over burden distribution and placement slowed the agreements down.

China pledged $41 billion to the pool at the BRICS leaders' summit in St. Petersburg in September 2013, $18 billion each from Brazil, India, and Russia, and $5 billion from South Africa. According to a BRICS official, China, which has the largest foreign exchange reserves in the world and contributes the most to the currency pool, wants a bigger managerial role. China likewise desires to host the reserve. "India and Brazil favor an equal division of the first funding. China wants more, as we are aware, "said a representative of Brazil." Despite this, there are no tensions at this time because we are still negotiating." Russian Finance Minister Anton Siluanov announced on October 11 that steps to establish a $100 billion fund to stabilize currency markets would be initiated in the first quarter of 2014. Guido

Mantega, Brazil's finance minister, promised that the fund would be established by March 2014. The deadline was moved to 2015 since, as of April 2014, neither the currency reserve pool nor the development bank had been established.

The fact that the current institutions primarily benefit non-BRICS corporations is one of the motivations for the BRICS development bank. It also has political significance because it enables BRICS member states to "promote their interests abroad... and can highlight the strengthening positions of countries whose opinion is frequently ignored by their developed American and European colleagues."

The BRICS Foreign Ministers met in March 2014 in The Hague on the sidelines of the Nuclear Security Summit, and they released a declaration that "noted the most recent media comment regarding the upcoming G20 Summit, scheduled to take place in Brisbane in November 2014. Each Member State has an equal claim to the G20's custody, and no Member State has the authority to decide the G20's nature or character on its own."

The Ministers noted that "The escalation of hostile language, sanctions and counter-sanctions, and force does not contribute to a sustainable and peaceful solution, according to international law, including the principles and purposes of the United Nations Charter," in reference to the tensions surrounding Russia's annexation of Ukrainian Crimea. This was in response to the earlier comment made by Julie Bishop, the current Australian Foreign Minister, who suggested that Russian President Vladimir Putin would not be allowed to attend the G20 Summit in Brisbane.

In a July 2014 article that concluded, "If the current trend continues, soon the dollar will be abandoned by most of the significant global economies and it will be kicked out of the global trade finance," the Governor of the Russian Central Bank, Elvira Nabiullina, claimed that the "BRICS partners promote the establishment of a system of multilateral swaps that will allow them to transfer resources to one or another country, if needed."

In the days leading up to the BRICS summit in Fortaleza, Brazil, on July 13, 2014, during the weekend of the FIFA World Cup's championship match, Russian President Vladimir Putin met with Brazilian President Dilma Rousseff to discuss and sign a number of bilateral agreements on air defense, gas, and education. The BRICS nations, which are among the biggest in the world, "cannot satisfy themselves in the middle of the 21st century with any form of dependency," according to Rouseff. The development bank and the monetary fund were unveiled at a BRICS meeting with the presidents of the Union of South American Nations in Brasilia after the Fortaleza summit. The monetary fund will have access to US$100 billion, while the development bank will have capital of US$50 billion, with each nation paying US$10 billion.

The BRICS nations' communications ministers agreed to work together in the field of information and communication technology by signing a memorandum of intent in August 2019. The sixth conference of the group's communication ministers, held in Brasilia, Brazil, saw the signing of this agreement. The Chinese-based New Development Bank intends to provide $15 billion to its member countries to support their faltering economies. The member nations anticipate a smooth return and the continuation of commercial trade prior to COVID-19. The

COVID-19 epidemic will be addressed at the summit they intend to hold virtually in St. Petersburg, Russia, along with how to modernize their international system.

The BRICS region has a mixed acceptance rate for the COVID-19 vaccination. Brazil and Russia are more skeptical of the vaccination than the other two, while China, India, and South Africa are the most receptive. Indian Prime Minister Narendra Modi demanded during the 13th BRICS summit that a transparent investigation into the causes of COVID-19 be conducted by the World Health Organization with "all countries'" full cooperation, and Chinese President Xi Jinping spoke immediately after, urging BRICS nations to "oppose politicization" of the process.

2.6 The ASEAN Organization

The Association of Southeast Asian Nations, or ASEAN, is a political and economic union with ten member states in Southeast Asia. It fosters intergovernmental cooperation and makes it easier for its members and other nations in the Asia-Pacific to all integrate economically, politically, militarily, educationally, and socioculturally. With a total area of 4,522,518 km2 (1,746,154 sq mi), the union is home to an estimated 668 million people.

The main goal of ASEAN was to hasten economic expansion, which would then hasten social advancement and cultural development. Promoting regional peace and stability based on the rule of law and the UN Charter was a secondary goal. With some of the world's fastest-growing economies, ASEAN has expanded its focus beyond the social and economic sectors. By deciding to create an ASEAN community with three pillars—the ASEAN Security Community, the ASEAN Economic Community, and the ASEAN Socio-Cultural Community—in 2003, ASEAN took a step toward emulating the European Union (EU). The ten rice stalks on the ASEAN flag and insignia stand for the ten Southeast Asian nations together in friendship.

When the foreign ministers of Indonesia, Malaysia, the Philippines, Singapore, and Thailand signed the ASEAN Declaration on August 8, 1967, ASEAN was officially established. As stated in the Declaration, the goals and objectives of ASEAN are to promote regional peace, cooperation, and mutual assistance on matters of common interest, to assist one another with training and research facilities, to work together for better utilization of agriculture and industry to raise the living standards of the people, to promote Southeast Asian studies, and to accelerate economic growth, social progress, and cultural development in the region.

To contain communism was the initial driving force behind the formation of ASEAN. With the occupation of the northern Korean peninsula by the Soviet Union after World War II, communist governments were established in North Korea (1945), the People's Republic of China (1949), and parts of the former French Indochina with North Vietnam (1954). These events were accompanied by the communist "Emergency" in British Malaya and unrest in the recently independent Philippines from the United States in the early 1950s.

As a "containment" extension and an eastern counterpart to the early defensive bulwark NATO in Western Europe of 1949, these events also encouraged the earlier formation of SEATO (South East Asia Treaty Organization), which was led by the United States and United Kingdom along with Australia and several Southeast Asian partners in 1954. A change in the balance of power following the fall of Saigon and the conclusion of the Vietnam War in April 1975, as well as the downfall of SEATO, allowed the local member nations of the ASEAN group to attain more coherence in the mid-1970s.

A number of industrial projects were approved at the inaugural ASEAN summit meeting, which took place in Bali, Indonesia, in 1976. A Treaty of Amity and Cooperation and a Declaration of Concord were also signed. After the Cold War ended, ASEAN nations were able to exercise more political independence in the area, and in the 1990s, ASEAN began to take the lead on matters relating to regional trade and security. The Southeast Asian Nuclear-Weapon-Free Zone Treaty was signed on December 15th, 1995, to make Southeast Asia a nuclear-weapon-free zone. After being accepted by all but one of the member nations, the treaty came into force on March 28, 1997. After the Philippines ratified it, it went into full effect on June 21, 2001, thus outlawing all nuclear weapons in the area.

Brunei joined ASEAN as its sixth member on January 7, 1984, and Vietnam joined as its seventh member on July 28,

1995, after the Cold War ended. On July 23, 1997, Laos and Myanmar (formerly Burma) united. A coup in 1997 and other domestic unrest prevented Cambodia from joining at the same time as Laos and Myanmar, delaying its membership. It rejoined on April 30, 1999, when its administration had stabilized.

Members of the charter, which was signed in November 2007, convened on December 15 in Jakarta to begin the process of creating "an EU-style community." The charter gave ASEAN legal status and attempted to unite the 500 million-person region into a single free-trade zone. Susilo Bambang Yudhoyono, the president of Indonesia, said: "This is a momentous development at a time when ASEAN is consolidating, integrating, and becoming a community.

It is accomplished at a time when the international order is undergoing a seismic shift, as ASEAN wants to play a more active role in Asian and global affairs. He concluded by stating that "Southeast Asia is no longer the brutally divided, war-torn area it was in the 1960s and 1970s," in reference to climate change and economic turmoil.

The purposes of the charter were perceived as being threatened by the financial crisis of 2007–2008, which also sparked the notion of a proposed human rights organization that would be debated at a summit in February 2009. This idea generated debate since the body would be ineffective because it lacked the authority to sanction or punish nations that infringed the rights of their citizens. Later in 2009, the organization was founded as the ASEAN Intergovernmental Commission on Human Rights (AICHR). The commission approved the ASEAN Human Rights Declaration in November 2012.

Chapter III. Future of Economic Progresses

Human capacity for innovation, modern technology, productivity and competitiveness, a sustainable environment, globalization, and the fourth industrial revolution will all be critical to economic progress in the future. However, the universal principles of global growth should be aimed at inclusiveness, sustainability, harmony, and shared responsibility. Chinese president Xi Jinping said that "a tree with strong and deep roots will grow well and better." The word "roots" probably he refers to the factors driving the national and global growth. In this chapter, you will learn the traces of economics from the past, present, and look into the future perspectives of economic progress.

3.1 Agricultural Revolution

The term "agricultural revolution" refers to a number of cultural shifts that originally made it possible for people to switch from a livelihood of hunting and gathering to one of agriculture and animal domestication. Less than a dozen crop species, many of which were domesticated many years ago, now make up more than 80% of the food consumed by humans globally.

To investigate the historical and contemporary effects of plant and animal domestication and to understand the reasons behind early cultivation practices, scientists examine ancient remains, bone artifacts, and DNA. The domestication of plants and animals began in different parts of the world starting in the Holocene epoch about 12 thousand years ago, most likely as a result of local population growth and climate change.

As people began to domesticate animals and then continued to choose plants and animals for desired features, the move from hunting and gathering to agriculture happened extremely gradually. A significant turning point in human history and evolution is the advent of agriculture. While human migration and trade fueled the expansion of agriculture around the world, the cultivation of plants and animals blossomed in a number of distinct domestication centers in accordance with the unique environmental circumstances of the location.

This shift in subsistence brought with it domesticated animals that could be used for meat and dairy products throughout the year, as well as surplus plant food that accumulated during the summer and fall for storage and winter consumption. The ability to form homesteads, towns, and communities allowed humans to stop moving around and migrating in search of food, which allowed them to quickly grow population densities and give rise to civilizations.

This reliance on domesticating plants and animals necessitated a variety of other environmental adaptations, such as deforestation, irrigation, and the setting aside of area for the cultivation of particular crops. Along with these other advances, it also led to the development of new tool technologies, trade, architecture, a more rigid division of labor, clear socioeconomic roles, property ownership, and multi-tiered political systems.

This change in the manner of subsistence gave people a comparatively safer way of life and, generally speaking, more free time for intellectual and artistic endeavors, which led to the formation of sophisticated languages and the rapid advancement of art, religion, and science. Increases in population density were linked to higher rates of illness, interpersonal conflict, and extreme socioeconomic stratification, though.

Modern humans are still being impacted by the development of agriculture, genetics, and society through changes in nutrition, an increased risk of obesity, and exposure to new diseases. This chapter will examine both the long-term beneficial and detrimental consequences of agriculture on society as well as the many regions that adopted early agricultural practices.

Between the mid-17th and late 19th centuries, increased labor and land productivity led to an unheard-of rise in agricultural production in Britain, which is known as the Agricultural Revolution. Up until 1770, agricultural productivity increased more quickly than population growth, and it afterwards continued to rank among the highest in the world. Although domestic food production was replaced by food imports in the 19th century as the population more than quadrupled to over 32 million, this rise in the food supply contributed to the quick growth of the population in England and Wales, from 5.5 million in 1700 to over 9 million by 1801.

A larger urban workforce, which was essential to industrialization, was created as a result of the gain in productivity, which hastened the decrease of the labor force's agricultural component. As a result, the Industrial Revolution has been linked to the Agricultural Revolution. Historians disagree about whether the events that led to the remarkable agricultural expansion could be considered "a revolution," as the increase was actually the consequence of a number of important improvements made over a lengthy period of time. As a result, it's unclear exactly when such a revolution occurred and what it was made of.

Less than a dozen crop species, many of which have been domesticated for many years, now make up more than 80% of the food consumed by humans globally. Archaeological evidence shows that, beginning in the Holocene epoch, the domestication of plants and animals arose in different parts of the world, most likely as a result of local population growth and climate change. A significant turning point in human history and evolution is the advent of agriculture.

3.2 Industrial Revolutions

The way people manufacture things is also altered by technological advancements. The industrial revolution is another name for the transition from pre-industrial technology to production technology. The working circumstances and lifestyles of individuals were dramatically altered by the new industrial technologies. What exactly were the industrial revolutions, and where are we now?

First Industrial Revolution

Through the use of steam power and the mechanization of industry, the First Industrial Revolution got its start in the 18th century. The mechanized version obtained eight times the volume in the same time as the basic spinning wheels that were previously used to create threads. The power of steam was well understood. The biggest innovation for raising productivity of people was using it for industrial reasons. Steam engines could be utilized to power weaving looms instead of human labor. Because people and products could travel enormous distances in shorter amounts of time, innovations like the steamship and (some 100 years later) the steam-powered locomotive brought about more significant improvements.

Second Industrial Revolution

The invention of electricity and the introduction of the assembly line marked the start of the Second Industrial Revolution in the 19th century. A slaughterhouse in Chicago, where pigs were strung from conveyor belts and each butcher only completed a portion of the slaughtering process, gave Henry Ford (1863–1947) the idea for mass production. Henry Ford applied these ideas to the manufacture of automobiles, fundamentally altering the industry. Previously, an entire automobile was put together at one station; now, vehicles are made in small batches on a conveyor belt, which is much faster and less expensive.

Third Industrial Revolution

The third industrial revolution, which started in the latter half of the 20th century with the adoption and widespread use of digital computers and digital record-keeping, is the transition from mechanical and analogue electronic technologies to digital electronics. It is still going on today. Implicitly, the phrase also alludes to the radical transformations that digital computing and communication technology brought about at this time. Since the development of these technologies, we have gained the ability to completely automate a production process without the use of humans. Robots that carry out preprogrammed sequences without human assistance are well-known examples of this.

Fourth Industrial Revolution

The Fourth Industrial Revolution is being put into practice right now. This is often referred to as "Industry 4.0" and is characterized by the use of information and communication technology in industry. It expands on the Third Industrial Revolution's advancements. A network link allows production systems with computer technology to be expanded and, in a sense, have a digital twin online. These enable the transmission of information about themselves and communication with other facilities. The next stage of factory automation is this. In "cyber-physical production systems," in which production systems, components, and people communicate via a network and production is essentially autonomous, the networking of all systems leads to smart factories. Industry 4.0 has the ability to bring forth some amazing advancements in manufacturing environments when these enablers come together. Examples include machines that can foresee problems and autonomously initiate repair procedures, or self-organized logistics that respond to unforeseen changes in production. Furthermore, it has the ability to alter how people conduct business. People may be drawn into smarter networks through Industry 4.0, which could lead to more productive working. The production environment has become more digitalized, which opens up more flexible ways to deliver the correct information to the right person at the right time. Maintenance workers may now receive equipment paperwork and service histories more quickly and at the point of use thanks to the growing use of digital devices in factories and out in the field. Maintenance specialists want to solve issues, not waste time looking for the necessary technical information.

Industry 4.0, in short, is revolutionary for all industrial settings. The production process will alter as a result of the digitalization of manufacturing, including how things are produced, delivered, and maintained. Given that, it can legitimately be said to mark the start of the fourth industrial revolution.

3.3 Innovation and Modern Technology

Income, employment, and quality of life all heavily depend on one's capacity to innovate and reap its rewards. Innovations not only help us achieve affluence, but they also play a growing role in resolving the numerous societal issues brought on by our pursuit of prosperity. Research-based expertise is becoming more and more crucial to the creation of new ideas and technologies. Understanding how and when research-based skills may promote prosperity and address social issues is crucial for creating effective innovation-focused R&D policy.

Innovation is the process of developing new goods, procedures, approaches, or services. By offering greater and/or more affordable functionality than the alternatives before, innovation adds value for the end customer. Changes in technology, business models, organizations, etc. are all part of innovation. A new company strategy, technology solution, or organizational change could all be the fundamental concept. To realize the maximum potential, however, modifications in all areas are frequently necessary. No firm can endure in a competitive economy for an extended period of time without upgrading its goods and services, or the processes by which they are made or provided. All business sectors must be encouraged to renew, and high tech businesses cannot be the sole focus of innovation policy.

Finding the ideal balance between competing demands is a crucial step in the innovation process because the majority of innovations are complex and each subsystem has its own limitations. Most of the time, there are multiple options for delivering a new function to users or for using a new technology. It is impossible to forecast with any degree of precision the feature combinations the market will favor. An innovation's final worth is also developed through adaptation and enhancement, frequently accumulated over many years. Innovation is best understood as an iterative, exploratory search process, regardless of whether the source was a market opportunity or a new technology capacity.

Technology, market, design, economics, and other sectors are all integrated into innovation. Having all the relevant skills in one organization is challenging. The costs are considerable, competency quickly ages out, and the business misses out on chances to gain insight from a wider range of experiences. As a result, innovation is now a continuous process of contact with clients—current or potential—suppliers and rivals, consultants, and academic researchers.

We refer to the patterns of mutual reliance and interaction between private and public entities as "innovation systems." The ability to innovate depends on how well the system's many components are integrated and tailored to one another.

In the past, new technology was created via real-world applications. Although it wasn't always necessary for the original innovation, a scientific grasp of how and why a technology functions has frequently paved the path for further advancements. Science and innovation are become increasingly interconnected and complexly entwined. Modern science is equally dependent on cutting-edge technology, but science-based innovations like microelectronics and biotechnology could not have been developed without scientific understanding.

Although there is no direct path from cutting-edge research to innovation, science-based competency plays a significant influence in industry's capacity to develop. Successful collaboration frequently relies more on the collective expertise of academic researchers than it does on the use of particular study findings.

Instead of being a quick burst of inspiration, innovation is a thorough search process that occurs both before and after a new product or technique is introduced. The search process might benefit greatly from research-based skills, but the first product idea is rarely the most significant contribution. Identifying long-term dangers and opportunities, as well as areas where a corporation needs to invest in new expertise, is a crucial strategic job.

The way that information is turned into new products or processes is how economists typically conceptualize innovation. Innovation is best described using a more fruitful metaphor as a process of exploratory learning where organizations and people acquire new skills. Their ability to compete with new goods, procedures, or business models is improved by this expertise.

3.4 International Trade and Cooperation

To eradicate poverty worldwide, trade is essential. Open economies tend to develop more quickly, innovate, increase productivity, and give their citizens more chances and higher incomes. By providing consumers with more cheap goods and services, open trade also benefits households with lower incomes. Economic growth and poverty reduction are aided locally and worldwide by integrating with the global economy through trade and global value chains.

The global economy has grown rapidly in recent decades. The even quicker increase in global trade has contributed to this expansion. Trade has increased as a result of both technology advancements and deliberate initiatives to lower trade obstacles. Many emerging nations haven't yet opened their economies to fully capitalize on the chances for economic growth through trade, but some have. Trade restrictions that still exist in industrialized nations are mostly focused on agricultural products and labor-intensive manufacturing, two industries where emerging nations have a comparative advantage. Increased trade liberalization in these sectors would benefit both industrialized and developing nations, helping the world's poorest people overcome the worst forms of poverty.

Countries' integration into the global economy has demonstrated to be a potent tool for fostering economic growth, development, and poverty reduction. World commerce has increased on average by 6% annually during the last 20 years, twice as quickly as global output. But commerce has fueled growth for a much longer. The world trading system has profited from eight rounds of multilateral trade liberalization since 1947, when the General Agreement on Tariffs and Trade (GATT) was established, as well as from unilateral and regional liberalization. In fact, the World Trade Organization was founded as a result of the final of these eight rounds—the so-called "Uruguay Round," which was finished in 1994—to help manage the expanding number of multilateral trade agreements.

The consequent global economic integration has improved living conditions all across the world. The majority of emerging nations have benefited from this prosperity, and in some, incomes have increased significantly. The importance of developing nations has increased significantly over time; they currently make approximately one-third of global trade, up from about a quarter in the early 1970s. In comparison to traditional commodity exports, many developing nations have significantly boosted their exports of manufactured goods and services: 80 percent of exports from developing nations now consist of manufactured goods. Furthermore, trade between emerging nations has expanded quickly; currently, 40 percent of their exports are made to other developing nations.

Integration has, nevertheless, made inconsistent progress in recent decades. For many developing nations in Asia and, to a lesser extent, in Latin America, progress has been very stunning. These nations have flourished as a result of their decision to engage in international trade, which has enabled them to draw the majority of foreign direct investment into developing nations. This is true of higher-income Asian nations like Korea and Singapore, who were themselves underdeveloped until the 1970s, as well as China and India, which have embraced trade liberalization and other market-oriented reforms.

However, many other nations, particularly those in Africa and the Middle East, have progressed more slowly. The world's poorest nations have seen their share of trade significantly decline, and if they don't lower their own trade barriers, they run the risk of being further marginalized. This category includes almost all of the least developed countries and about 75 developing and transitional economies. They rely disproportionately on the production and export of traditional commodities, as opposed to the successful integrators. Their marginalization is caused by a variety of factors, including ingrained structural issues, ineffective institutional and regulatory frameworks, and protection both domestically and internationally.

For sustainable economic growth, policies that open up an economy to trade and investment with the rest of the globe are required. Clear evidence supports this. No nation has recently seen economic success in the sense of appreciable rises in the standard of life for its citizens without being open to the rest of the world. In contrast, East Asia's economic growth has been significantly influenced by trade opening (along with opening to foreign direct investment), as the region's average import tariff has decreased from 30% to 10% during the past 20 years.

In order for many emerging nations to gain competitive advantages in the production of certain goods, they had to open their economies to the global economy. Over 120 million (14%) fewer people lived in absolute poverty in these nations, which the World Bank refers to as "new globalizers," between 1993 and 1998. There is strong evidence that nations with a stronger global outlook consistently experience quicker economic growth than their domestic counterparts. In fact, one result suggests that the advantages of trade liberalization can outweigh the disadvantages by a factor of more than ten. India, Vietnam, and Uganda are three nations that have recently opened their economy and have seen faster development and greater reductions in poverty. In general, emerging nations that drastically reduced their tariffs in the 1980s expanded faster in the 1990s than those that did not.

Free commerce frequently benefits everyone, but notably the impoverished. The substantial implicit subsidies that trade protection offers, which are frequently directed to select privileged interests, are beyond the means of developing nations. Additionally, the enhanced growth brought about by freer trade itself has the tendency to raise the incomes of the poor in a manner that is roughly equivalent to that of the general population. Unskilled employees are given new opportunities to work, moving them into the middle class. Since 1990, global inequality has been declining, a trend that can be attributed in part to developing nations' faster economic growth as a result of trade liberalization.

The benefits from removing residual trade restrictions are significant. Gains from removing all trade restrictions on goods are predicted to be between $250 billion and $680 billion annually. The industrialized nations would receive about two thirds of these benefits. However, the benefit to poor nations would still be greater than twice as much as the amount of help they currently receive. Furthermore, because their economies are more heavily protected and are subject to greater hurdles, developing nations would benefit from global trade liberalization more as a percentage of their GDP than industrial countries.

Even if increased access to markets in other nations has advantages, governments gain the most from liberalizing their own markets. The deregulation of their agricultural markets would be the key gain for industrialized nations. Agriculture and manufacturing sector liberalization would benefit developing nations essentially equally. However, because to the greater relative importance of agriculture in their economy, the group of low-income nations would benefit the most from agricultural liberalization in industrial countries.

3.5 The Better World and Better Government

The world has experienced significant social advancements and technological advancement over the last 30 years. Unprecedented economic progress has occurred, helping hundreds of millions of people escape poverty. We are gaining from a profound digital transformation that has the potential to address some of our most serious social and environmental issues. Nevertheless, despite these achievements, our current development paradigm has serious flaws.

The markets of today are filled with indications of its shortcomings and failure. Since the 1980s, the number of climate change-related natural disasters has doubled. In 2014, lost biodiversity and ecological damage cost the globe an estimated 3% of GDP, while violence and armed conflict cost the equivalent of 9% of GDP.

We keep making investments in high-carbon infrastructure at a rate that puts us at risk of catastrophic, irreversible climate change. Globally, social inequality and youth unemployment are getting worse, and women are still paid on average 25% less than males for similar labor.

Since the 1980s, median real earnings have remained unchanged in developed economies due to a combination of strong opposition to further globalization, deep concern about how automation will affect both service and manufacturing sectors. While total debt remains uncomfortably high, real interest rates are historically low or even negative in several major nations. The outlook on the economy oscillates erratically between techno-optimism and political pessimism.

The Global Goals for Sustainable Development

A world that is fully sustainable would be one that is socially just, environmentally secure, economically wealthy, inclusive, and more predictable. As long as firms work together to achieve them, they offer a workable framework for long-term success.

Progress on all of the goals will have a significantly greater impact than attaining just some because they are all meant to interact. Naturally, the results won't be heaven on earth; there will be a lot of real-world difficulties. But without a question, things would be better and more robust. We might be creating a system of abundance. Leaders in business will undoubtedly support these outcomes. But given that half of businesspeople believe this is government territory, they are less likely to feel accountable for delivering them.

Our analysis paints a totally different picture. First, it demonstrates how crucial the Global Goals are for business, as they provide an inspiring growth plan for each company, for the industry as a whole, and for the global economy. The abundance the Global Goals promise won't materialize unless private businesses seize the market possibilities they create and drive progress on the entire package of Global Goals.

The Commission members who run businesses have made the decision to integrate the Sustainable Development Goals into our basic growth goals, value chain operations, and policy stances. Regardless of the size of their operations, this research contends that other corporate executives should take the same action quickly.

You can take the following six steps as a business leader to win your part of the reward, according to the Commission. Real leadership at the top is required for all of them in order to motivate employees to work with passion and dedication and to change the marketplaces in which you all compete.

1. Encourage your firms and the rest of the business community to support the Global Goals as the best growth strategy. The sooner we move toward better business in a better society, the more business leaders will comprehend the business case for the Global Goals.

2. Integrate firm strategy with the global goals. This entails viewing all aspects of strategy through the lens of the Global Goals, including selecting board members and senior executives to prioritize and drive execution, focusing strategic planning and innovation on sustainable solutions, encouraging consumers to make sustainable choices through marketing products and services, and using the goals to direct leadership development, women's empowerment at all levels, regulatory policy, and capital allocation. By 2030, there will be 380 million additional

employment thanks to the Global Goals. In addition to your immediate activities, you must ensure that all additional employment you create will pay a livable wage and are decent jobs. This applies not only to your supply chains and distribution networks. Additionally, you must assist investors in comprehending the magnitude of value that sustainable business may generate.

3. Lead sector peers in driving the transition to sustainable markets. The Global Goals will be more fully realized if entire industries are put on a sustainable foundation, creating considerably larger business prospects. Think about agriculture and food. A global food and agriculture system that supports the Global Goals would provide a growing global population with wholesome, affordable food, increase earnings for the 1.5 billion small farmers worldwide, and support the restoration of forests, freshwater supplies, and important ecosystems. By 2030, it would add additional economic value of more than US$2 trillion. 12 Furthermore, it would be far more resistant to climate risk. This market revolution cannot be achieved by

conducting business as usual. Furthermore, the shift cannot be fueled by a few sustainable innovators using disruptive innovation; the entire industry must change. By identifying tipping points, prioritizing key technological and policy levers, creating new skill profiles and jobs, quantifying the need for new financing, and outlining the components of a just transition, forward-thinking business leaders are laying out their collective path to a sustainable competitive playing field. Driving system transformation with sector peers in line with the Global Goals will be a crucial, differentiating talent for a world-class business leader over the next 15 years. It include creating new opportunities, identifying potential sources of disruption, and renewing company licenses.

4. Collaborate with decision-makers to cover the real cost of using natural and human resources. To use business jargon, internalizing externalities means that all competitors must pay prices that accurately reflect the underlying costs of the way they conduct their operations. Pricing pollution at its actual societal and environmental

costs has long been a notion. To combat the risk of uncontrollable climate change, however, the need for robust carbon price is becoming more and more important. The start of a "race to the top" is signaled by setting pricing for carbon as well as other natural resources (particularly water in many locations) and upholding those prices. To avoid being at a cost disadvantage, companies that opt to pay living wages and the full cost of their resources must be certain that their rivals will do the same in the not-too-distant future. To implement fiscal and regulatory policies that level the playing field and are more in line with the Global Goals, business leaders must collaborate freely with regulators, business, and civil society. This could entail making fiscal systems more progressive by increasing taxes on pollution and unfairly priced resources while decreasing taxes on labor income.

5. Advocate for a financial structure that encourages sustainable investment over the long term. The estimated US$2.4 trillion in additional investment needed each year, particularly for infrastructure and other projects with

lengthy payback periods, is necessary to achieve the Global Goals. There is enough money on hand. However, given the unpredictability of the world, most investors seek liquidity and quick returns. Investors will primarily rely on a company's financial performance to assess how well it is performing in relation to the Global Goals once corporations start charging "full" pricing that account for social and environmental externalities. The economy will need some time to reach full prices, though. Business leaders can increase the amount of capital flowing into sustainable investments by advocating for three things: transparent, standardized league tables of sustainability performance linked to the Global Goals; broader and more effective use of blended finance instruments to share risk and draw significantly more private capital into sustainable infrastructure; and alignment of regulatory reforms in the financial sector with long-term goals.

6. Reconstruct the Social Contract Since the global financial crisis, trust in business has declined so dramatically that the social fabric is fraying. Many believe that business has

broken the social contract. By collaborating with governments, citizens, workers, and civil society to accomplish the full spectrum of Global Goals and by engaging in responsible, transparent policy advocacy, business leaders can reclaim society's trust and secure their right to operate. Businesses must pay their taxes publicly, like everyone else, in order to rebuild the social contract, and they must give back to the communities where they operate. Over 700 million people are employed directly and indirectly across the world's supply networks. A more inclusive society and larger consumer markets may be created by treating them with respect and paying them a living wage. Higher labor productivity would result from investing in their education, allowing both men and women to reach their full potential. Additionally, it should be unavoidable to ensure that the social contract extends from the formal into the informal sectors by fully implementing the UN Guiding Principles on Business and Human Rights. Over 150 million children are still working in the fields, mines, workshops, and garbage dumps that support a large portion of the global economy, both seen and unprotected, along with 20 to 40 million other people who are engaged in some sort of modern slavery.

Chapter V. The Education and Peace

4.1 Life's Lessons from the US Navy Seal

The US Navy Special Force, called the Navy Seals, is considered one of the most powerful armies in the world and only used for major operations when the task is beyond the capabilities of the regular army. This army is selected from among the best armies and trained more intensively. That is the hardest and most rigorous training to become a great warrior. This team not only trains the body to be strong, powerful, and agile, but also the mind, spirit, strength, discipline, and fearlessness in the face of a wide range of the most dangerous situations. The Navy Zeal can teach you the following lessons about life:

1. They have to get up in the morning, and the coach will check first and foremost to make sure their beds are arranged in the most orderly manner. They absolutely must prepare the bed and other materials well. Everything must be perfect. "What a great fighter for an unusual operation, but instead have to prepare the most beautiful place to sleep, maybe a special operation on the bed," the soldiers would laugh at first. But it is only

when they follow through regularly that they realize they have changed the most. Every morning, after you wake up, you must complete a task that is required to prepare the best possible environment. No procrastination, no mental languidness. You must be able to do small things well before you can accomplish a great task. You need to teach yourself to be alert and determined to do well from the beginning.

2. In coaching, army is divided into groups of seven. Each team must have a boat to be pushed, and that boat would cross the sea across the ice at a great distance. In order to reach the destination, everyone must work together to pull, push, and paddle with all their strength and make sure to get the boat back to the seashore. This means that in order to be successful, you have to work as a team, you have to work hard together, if someone does not work hard, they will not be able to reach the goal and will be eliminated from training. You have to work together, have a team spirit, take responsibility for the

fate of the team, and take care of each other. Want to succeed, you cannot do it alone.

3. Out of 150 soldiers, only 35 will be selected. During the training session of Admiral William McRavin, he said, "All the trainers are the fastest runners, the fastest swimmers, the fastest rowers, and the fastest climbers, and they are strong and hefty." "One of them was the smallest, and he was always laughed at and thought he would be fired in the next episode." However, in all the tests set up—running, pushing, rowing, and climbing walls—the short man always wins first place. In this training, the most fair and equitable thing is that no matter who you are, no matter what color you are, no matter how small you are, as long as you work hard, you will win. It is also a point that tells you that you cannot look at people from the outside; you must look at their real abilities. Don't judge the book by its cover.

4. Every morning, if you do not prepare your bed properly or dress modestly, you will be subjected to one of the strictest penalties: you must run as fast as you can across

the desert, through the deep mud, and dive deep, bury yourself in the mud, keep your head down, and recover. You need to do this all day long. All trainees are punished like this. In this case, no matter how hard you try, the coach will find any small weakness of yours to punish. The lesson here is that no matter how good you are, it is impossible to please everyone, especially the faultfinders. So you have to acknowledge any wrongdoing, accept the punishment (criticism), and move on.

5. During the training, each trainee will be tested on a number of challenging issues, such as long-distance running, long-distance swimming, exercise, and long-distance lifting, crawling under thorns, climbing mountains, hand-tied swimming, tying your legs, and doing a lot of other things to keep you physically and mentally fit to continue this work. Failure means injury. At this stage, whoever wants to stop wanting to give up is not forced, but if you stop, you will not be able to become the special team as a great warrior. This is a test

of how well you can deal with the most difficult situations. Everyone who can do it will be strong and energetic. The lesson from this point is that life is not easy. If you want to be strong, you have to train and face many difficult problems because life is full of pain, discouragement, despair, and problems at every turn. If you give up, you will return to your normal self, but if you persevere, you will become a superhuman. Your life is up to you; whether you want to give up or struggle is up to you. No one forces you.

6. All soldiers will go through dangerous training after undergoing strenuous training that requires both physical and mental strength. You may think it is the craziest training, but it must be done if you want to move forward. That is training to swim in San Diego Island, an area rich in white sharks. The trainer will describe the beauty of the coral and other aquatic species before the training begins. But at the same time, you will face a shark that will come and eat you. However, research has established how to deal with this shark. Before it attacks

you, the shark will swim around you. To resist this shark, you must not be afraid of it. You must look at it firmly, take up your position, gather strength to escape, and hit it in the nose; it will run away. The lesson here is that in a world full of sharks, critics, discourage, and spread negative thoughts and prejudices. You do not have to be afraid of such people, you have to concentrate and move forward or fight back as best you can.

7. Naval Special Forces training focuses on attacking enemy ships on the seabed. During training, the soldier had to dive into the water and swim to the enemy fleet at night, which was almost 4 kilometers away, equipped with a respirator. You can see some light while swimming to the enemy ship, but when you get to the ship in training, you will be in the darkest situation. The goal is to reach the bottom of the ship, which is the deepest point and also the most dangerous. In such a dark and dangerous situation, the Zeal must concentrate calmly and use his trained skills to reach the ship's bottom. The lesson we can learn from this is that when

life encounters the worst and darkest problems, you must concentrate to find the light again. You have to remember that the more difficult the problem, the more you have to calm down.

4.2 The Declining of Russia

Putin will witness the collapse of his life's work, and the six things you should know about the war in Ukraine.

1. Like Nazi Germany, revanchist, imperialist, genocidal, and fascist Russia is a world power. Our expectations that Russia will eventually achieve some kind of domestic normalcy and foreign harmony have been dashed by the Russo-Ukrainian War. Famously, Ronald Reagan described to the Soviet Union as a "evil empire." It's possible that the Russian Federation is an even worse terrible would-be empire. While existing empires are typically content with the status quo, aspiring empires grow and launch wars. Russia's conflict with Ukraine cannot be won, but it can only be put an end to once and for all if Russia gives up its revanchist, imperialist, genocidal, and fascist tendencies. Negotiations will be

fruitless, and only defeat will be able to fundamentally alter how Russia interacts with its neighbors and the rest of the world.

2. Vladimir Putin, the president of Russia, may or may not be mentally unstable, but he is unquestionably a mediocre chess player, not the magnificent master he was described as being. Putin has managed to alienate Russia's friends and allies, turn Russia into a severely corrupt and ineffective petro-state, destroy the market economy and its professional classes, tarnish Russia's reputation by connecting it with war crimes, and involve it in a disastrous war that will go down in history as one of the biggest strategic errors. All of this has been accomplished in his more than 20 years in power. But Putin's biggest error might have been to establish himself as the centerpiece and fulcrum of the Russian political system. Russians will find it difficult to view him as the embodiment of their country as he ages. And the system will struggle to function without him when he departs, which he will undoubtedly do.

3. The Russian army is in disarray, just like the Russian government, society, economy, and culture. Evidently, Putin's allies stole the funds intended to finance its refurbishment. Its armaments and heavy equipment are far worse than anyone could have anticipated, and its tactics, strategy, and command and control are outdated. Russian society is in a serious crisis as millions of middle-class professionals have left the Putin dictatorship in search of better opportunities abroad, while others who are unable or unwilling to go are seeing their possibilities reduced by a weakening economy.

4. The world has been surprised by the resilience, bravery, and devotion to democracy and freedom displayed by Ukrainians and their president, Volodymyr Zelensky, as well as by their capacity to withstand and then push back the Russian assault. Putin's invasion, slaughter, and war could not have been fought off by a corrupt and severely fractured nation, as was the image of Ukraine prior to the war, which wears down its Western backers. Despite their propensity to gripe, Ukrainians are undoubtedly

loyal to their nation, regardless of where they reside or what language they speak.

5. Western analysts and politicians drastically miscalculated Zelensky, Putin, and the Ukraine. Despite the fact that Western military, financial, and humanitarian aid to Ukraine proved crucial to its capacity to push the Russians back, at the outset of the conflict, the West judged Russia to be stronger, Putin to be more competent, Ukraine to be weaker, and Zelensky to be incompetent. Therefore, it is important to take the West's predictions of what would happen in the event of a Russian collapse with a grain of salt. Much of Eurasia could experience a prolonged bloodbath similar to what happened following Imperial Russia's fall. However, a peaceful disintegration of the Russian Federation like to that of the Soviet Union is also a possibility.

6. In any case, a Ukrainian loss would be disastrous for peace, security, democracy, and liberalism in general and for Eurasia in particular because it would mark the triumph of revanchism, imperialism, genocide, and war.

A Ukrainian triumph, on the other hand, would be a death blow to everything Putin and his allies and fans believe in.

7. If 2022 provides any indication of what to expect in 2023, we may anticipate that Ukraine will continue to win wars and that Russia will experience more domestic and international problems.

8. 2023 may easily turn into a rerun of 1917, when a lost war, a collapsing economy, public unrest, the ruler's incompetence, and elite illegitimacy led to the end of Russia, as the Ukrainians must fight for their country's life while the Russians do not. Will Putin witness the failure of his entire life's work?

4.3 What to Watch for in 2023?

1. Global Economy: Due to prolonged inflation that is probably reducing, global economic growth is anticipated to slow down in 2019. With the possible exception of China, the main economies will lose the economic benefit from easing Covid-19 limitations. Major central banks will continue tightening monetary policy to combat inflation while governments won't be implementing significant stimulus measures. In October, the International Monetary Fund predicted that, aside from the global financial crisis in 2009 and the initial Covid-19 shock in 2020, global GDP growth would fall to 2.7 percent in 2023 from 3.2 percent in 2022.

2. U.S. Economic Statecraft in Asia: The success of the Indo-Pacific Economic Framework for Prosperity (IPEF), a policy initiative of the Biden administration, will be put to the test in the following year, along with the White House's larger economic and Asia-related policies. As the administration looks to produce at least some tangible results before mid-November, when President Biden will welcome other leaders of the Asia-Pacific Economic Cooperation (APEC) forum to San Francisco for their annual summit, the pace of IPEF talks is likely to pick up after the first full round of negotiations in Brisbane this month.

3. Export restrictions on technology: Over the course of the upcoming year, export restrictions will become more prevalent as the Biden administration places a greater emphasis on safeguarding and advancing vital technologies in the context of escalating strategic competition with China. The Biden administration issued export restrictions on October 7 in an effort to prevent China from obtaining cutting-edge semiconductors and the machinery needed to create them. The action signified a paradigm shift in U.S. export control strategy: controls would now be utilized to assure the United States maintained "as large of a lead as possible," rather than allowing rivals to advance technologically at a safe distance behind it.

4. Infrastructure and Development Finance Policy: The Partnership for Global Infrastructure and Investment (PGII), IPEF, the Blue Dot Network (BDN), the Trilateral Infrastructure Partnership (TIP), and the Quadrilateral Security Forum are just a few of the infrastructure-related initiatives that will continue to be a central part of the Biden administration's foreign policy in 2023. (Quad). These initiatives aim to rival China's Belt and Road Initiative while also raising the bar for good infrastructure.

5. Climate Finance: Expect increased efforts in 2023 to increase investment in climate mitigation and adaptation globally, as the Inflation Reduction Act has mobilized investment in clean energy domestically. The funding and operation of the "loss and damage fund," which was unveiled at the UN Climate Change Conference (COP27) last month, as well as the fund's connection to the Paris Agreement's climate finance commitments, as well as the function of international financial institutions in financing for climate and other "global public goods," remain major open questions. The multilateral development banks are being urged by many shareholders and outside experts to increase lending and promote greater private investment, notably in the context of Just Energy Transition Partnerships (JETPs).

4.4 Four Things to Review in 2022

1. Covid-19 Economics: The unanticipated Russia-Ukraine war and the repercussions of the Covid-19 epidemic prevented the world economy from fully recovering. In contrast to its initial forecast of 4.9%, the

IMF now expects growth to ultimately reach 3.2%. Inflation is most likely to be the economic narrative that defines 2022. Prices in the West increased faster than they had in any other region since the early 1980s. All economies faced challenges from weakened supply networks, but the major factors causing core inflation diverged on either side of the Atlantic. Strong demand for durable goods and a robust labor market in the United States were the main factors driving inflation. Inflation was a result of rising costs, wages, and job growth across the country. Pandemic supply shocks in Europe were the primary cause of inflation, which was then made worse by Russia's conflict in Ukraine. All year long, the cost of food and energy rose dramatically, which raised other prices. Because of this, even when jobs started to return, labor markets throughout Europe found it difficult to support wage growth. The "Zero-Covid" strategy in China hindered a domestic recovery and made the world's problems worse. Beijing set a growth goal of 5% in March, but the OECD currently predicts that China will only expand by roughly

3.3%. In contrast to expectations, consumption in retail and industry lagged. Lockdowns are disruptive to daily life and weaken the already fragile real estate market.

2. U.S. Indo-Pacific Strategy: This year, the White House's policy department was kept busy with the creation of the country's Indo-Pacific strategy. The White House published its concise Indo-Pacific Strategy in February, which outlines the administration's plans to reshape the area through a "latticework" of alliances. Although the Indo-Pacific Economic Framework (IPEF), which held its first ministerial in September, is at the center of this strategy's economic agenda, other smaller agreements, such as the Quad's Critical and Emerging Technology Working Group and Chip Four, are still taking shape. The first National Security Strategy from the White House, which was released in October, claims that China is "America's most critical geopolitical issue" and that it wants to have a "increased sphere of influence" in the Indo-Pacific. The surprise signing of a security agreement in April between China and the Solomon Islands set off alarm bells in Washington, and the Pacific Islands became center stage for U.S. strategy. A wide economic and security agreement between China and eleven Pacific Island countries came to a standstill in May due to opposition from states like Fiji, which expressed its reluctance to China's aspirations by joining IPEF. In September, the Biden administration conducted the first-ever summit between the United States and Pacific Island nations and released a Pacific Partnership Strategy to go along with it. Competition between the United States and China: As expected, the year in competition between the United States and China was characterized by a blurred line separating economic security from national security. The administration's policy to China, as outlined by Secretary of State Antony Blinken in May, involves "investing" in domestic technical competitiveness, "aligning" with allies on economic norms, and "competing" with China economically. The CHIPS and Science Act was passed by the US government in order to invest in and support the domestic semiconductor industry. On the ally front, the US and its thirteen partner nations started IPEF negotiations and deepened their relationship with one another. On the competitive front, the Biden administration implemented new export restrictions on China in October, launching a new strategy for managing technology rivalry. Additionally, the government added 21 businesses from China's AI chip industry and the leader in memory chips, YMTC, on the BIS entity list in December. This year, competition was mostly a one-way highway as the Chinese government focused on preserving stability before the 20th Party Congress, which ultimately saw Xi Jinping solidify his position and win a third term as General Secretary of the Chinese Communist Party. The administration was also engaged with fighting Covid-19. The latter involved handling broad resentment over the Zero-Covid policy and securing Shanghai for more than two months. Tensions between the United States and China reached its pinnacle this year in July and August due to U.S. House Speaker Nancy Pelosi's visit to Taiwan, which was her first since 1997. China conducted military drills that were unprecedented in scope and near to Taiwan after Pelosi left the island.

3. Digital Currencies: The year 2022 saw more research into central bank digital currencies (CBDCs). A report outlining the advantages and disadvantages of a U.S. CBDC, a move that might "fundamentally transform the U.S. financial system," was published by the Federal Reserve Board in January. Despite worries about the instability of money flows, consumer vulnerability, and the creation of globally coordinated laws to assure interoperability, the concept has gained popularity. Over 100 nations are considering the creation of CBDCs, a 50 percent rise since May 2020, thanks to advancements in global technology and a decline in the use of cash. Ten nations have fully launched their digital currency projects, while the majority are still in the research phase. China's CBDC trial is scheduled to begin in 2023. The year 2022 in the world of crypto currencies was one of instability. Beginning in early February, a flourishing crypto currency business made headlines with a Super Bowl advertising blitz. The May Bitcoin crash, a significant reset that rocked the crypto currency sector and so-called stable coins—crypto assets intended to be stable through their relationship to fiat currencies—instead increased market volatility. With the bankruptcy of well-known crypto currency exchange FTX in November, investor confidence in crypto currencies fell even further. Market instability, disgruntled investors, and increased requests for regulation were all results of the collapse of FTX. With the signing of President Biden's executive order to create a strategy for digital assets, such as crypto currencies and CBDCs, that safeguards investors and consumers, U.S. crypto regulation did advance. The EO's main objective is to reduce the risks associated with digital transactions while maximizing the opportunity for U.S. leadership in the world market.

4. Orbital infrastructure: The deployment of the James Webb Space Telescope, the NASA Artemis 1 launch, and the ongoing CNSA Tiangong space station construction are just a few of the major breakthroughs in space news that occurred this year. Significant improvements were made in the area of low Earth orbit (LEO) infrastructure, which is a little bit closer to all of us here on Earth. More than 700,000 members currently receive satellite internet access from SpaceX's Starlink program, which has continuing to expand. As it develops its own constellation of LEO facilities, China launched three test satellites successfully in May (although not all of China's launches this year were successful). The U.S. GAO released a report criticizing the environmental impact of satellite constellations; Amazon postponed the launch of its Project Kuiper satellites until 2023; China and Russia voiced concerns about Starlink's potential military capabilities; and a geomagnetic storm destroyed 40 Starlink satellites. The Russian invasion of Ukraine was arguably the largest development in orbital infrastructure this year. The cooperation on the development of orbital infrastructure was also hampered by Western nations' efforts to economically and diplomatically isolate Russia. As a result of Starlink's quick post-invasion installation of satellite internet service in Ukraine, Kyiv is currently expanding its selection of satellite internet providers. Internet satellites were launched by SpaceX for service provider OneWeb after a planned launch from Russia was postponed in the early weeks of March. While the United States called for a halt to the testing of anti-satellite missile systems, and a December United Nations resolution backed that request, Russia has maintained its contentious testing. As more infrastructure is put in place, low Earth orbit is expected to becoming increasingly crowded. As a result, governments, armies, scientists, and environmental activists will all be paying more attention to the problem.

4.5 Southeast Asia Aspirations for the Future EV Hub

Many nations are looking to electric vehicles (EVs) as a means of lowering carbon emissions as they work to meet their climate commitments. A window of opportunity for EV production has opened up due to global attempts to diversify supply chains and the need to adopt green technologies, particularly in Southeast Asia. By 2025, 20% of all vehicles in the region will be electric, according to the International Renewable Energy Agency, and there is much more room for expansion given the region's population of over 680 million people and growing middle class. The nations of Southeast Asia are making noteworthy efforts to position their domestic industries as a crucial component of the EV ecosystem by creating materials that support supply chain resilience and putting in place economic regulations that encourage domestic adoption.

1. **Manufacturing of batteries:** By 2028, it is anticipated that the Indo-Pacific EV battery market would reach a value of over $90 billion. Southeast Asia presents a compelling alternative for nations like the United States that want to improve their supply chains for cutting-edge technologies and reduce their reliance on China. Although China presently supplies 50% of the materials used in battery refinement and about 75% of all lithium-ion batteries, Indonesia is ideally positioned to become a hub for battery manufacture as it is home to the greatest nickel, tin, and copper reserves in the world. Joko "Jokowi" Widodo, the president of Indonesia, recently urged his nation to create an "industry ecosystem for lithium batteries" in order to

accomplish this goal. The government forbade the export of nickel ore in 2020 in anticipation of the rising need for batteries. Indonesia opened its first EV battery manufacturing facility in Central Java in June 2022, complete with upstream and downstream battery production components. With plans to begin mass producing battery cells in 2024, South Korean companies LG Energy Solution and Hyundai Motors have also just started building an EV battery facility in Indonesia. Vietnam is a top destination for the manufacture of batteries due to its extensive nickel reserves. The largest private business in Vietnam, Vinfast, is building a factory to make 100,000 EV batteries annually for sale and internal use. Vietnam's capacity as a manufacturing hub will increase with the localization of supply chains, and the country will likely become a more appealing investment target due to Vinfast's reputation. Southeast Asia's potential has also been recognized by other foreign businesses. While Malaysia's Hong Seng Consolidated Berhad and EoCell inked an MOU in June 2022 to build a regional EV battery manufacturing hub in Malaysia, China's CATL and Taiwan's Foxconn are also considering investing in Indonesia's ambitions to lead battery production.

2. **Export Manufacturing:** The expansion of production for export is another indication that Southeast Asian nations are getting ready to move on to the next phase of EV production. By 2025, Indonesia wants to export 200,000 electric vehicles, or around 20% of all the cars it exports. In May 2022, Indonesian Investment Minister Bahlil Lahadalia revealed that the country had a contract with Tesla to establish a battery and electric vehicle plant in Central Java. Vinfast's efforts are representative of Vietnam's emphasis on integrating emerging technology with its production capabilities and its ambition to become a significant participant in the EV industry. Vinfast is both rapidly growing internationally and has its own EV manufacturing facilities in the nation with a capacity to produce about 950,000 EVs annually. As part of its strategy to sell its first EVs in the United States this year, it has revealed plans to invest $2 billion to start EV

manufacturing in North Carolina and $200 million to build a U.S. headquarters in Los Angeles. Operationally speaking, this decision makes sense given that Vietnam's main export market and second-largest trade partner is the United States, which is also the second-largest automobile market in the world. Additionally, Vinfast has disclosed plans to increase its sales to at least 50 locations across Europe.

3. Promoting both domestic adoption and foreign investment financial incentives to draw foreign investment are another weapon in the region's toolbox for becoming a recognized EV hub. Many nations' economic and sustainable development objectives now include increased EV adoption and production. In order to strengthen the nation's competitive advantage, the Thai government has named "Next Generation Automotive" as one of its 10 S-Curve Industries. The government declared in February 2022 that it will lower import charges for fully constructed EVs by 20 to 40 percent and lower excise taxes on imported EVs from 8 to 2 percent. Incentives, such as a reduction in the

income tax from 35 percent to 17 percent, are used in conjunction with these policies to entice competent foreign workers to work in the targeted industries. Similar incentives have been put in place in Singapore to promote domestic adoption. As a result of the Transport Ministry's 2021 rebate program, which reduced the upfront cost of buying an EV by around $31 million, the percentage of EV registrations rose from 0.2 percent in 2020 to 4.4 percent in 2021. To satisfy anticipated demand, the Land Transport Authority has set a goal of establishing 60,000 charging sites around the island by 2030. According to Cambodia's Long-Term Strategy for Carbon Neutrality, by the year 2050, 40% of cars and 70% of motorcycles will be electric vehicles. Additionally, in 2021, the government cut import taxes on EVs so that they would be roughly 50% lower than those on conventional automobiles. Following suit, Malaysia and the Philippines have implemented laws exempting EV makers from income taxes for four to seven years in the Philippines and exempting EV owners from paying road tax in Malaysia.

4. **EVs and Southeast Asia's Energy Security:** Despite environmental concerns, Southeast Asian nations' efforts to grow their domestic EV industries have a negative influence on the region's energy security, particularly in light of the current crisis between Russia and Ukraine. As gas prices have risen, the cost of making an EV battery and buying an EV has decreased over time, giving them a competitive edge. According to the Sixth ASEAN Energy Outlook (AEO6), which was published in 2020, the region's overall final energy consumption is predicted to rise by 146% by 2040, in part due to rising transportation demand. However, the promotion of EVs would result in an 18% reduction in energy demand in the transportation sector under a model scenario if ASEAN member states' national climate targets were met. The absence of a reliable fossil fuel-free electrical system and charging infrastructure continues to be Southeast Asia's biggest barrier to the expansion of the EV industry. However, numerous nations are making efforts to increase the number of available charging stations. Southeast Asian nations

should be encouraged to improve their energy security since rising inflation and commodities prices are endangering the region's political and economic stability. EVs could pave the way.

Chapter V. Conclusion and Recommendation

1. Conclusion

The situation of the global economy and politics has always been in flux. The world has always swung back and forth between good and evil, peace and war, growth and decline, competition and cooperation, stability and instability. However, uncertainty and skepticism will always exist in global politics and the economy. In politics and economy, we are now living in the age of globalization, international organization, international system, international order, and international cooperation. However, the competition for natural resources, supremacy, market dominance, supremacy in technology and science, supremacy in geopolitics, between superpowers, rich and poor, developed and developing countries, is causing extremely serious concerns for the political and economic sustainability and future of our planet.

In the final decades of the 20th century, the world underwent significant change. At the close of the 1980s, the Cold War came to an end, ushering in a time of significant political and economic transformation. In terms of politics and economics, the United States has emerged as the lone superpower. The U.S. dollar, which is its official currency, serves as the de facto global reserve currency for the pricing of commodities, energy, and international investments. While it continued to be the leader in innovation, its debt was sought after worldwide as a secure investment.

However, other fundamental structural changes were also taking place at the same time, most notably the development of developing economies like China. China went from being one of the world's lowest economies in 1980 to becoming the second largest in little about three decades. The shift in the weight of the global economy in the twenty-first century is mostly due to the speed and scale of Chinese expansion.

China and the United States have been the "twin engines" of economic expansion ever since. Following the global financial crisis a decade ago, developing economies now account for a greater share of global economic growth than advanced ones, signaling the end of American economic hegemony and the emergence of a dual or multi-polar world.

Early in the 1990s, by adopting opening and marketization, emerging nations were brought back into the global economy, profoundly altering its structure. These changes occurred at the same time as important institutional reforms in the advanced countries, such as financial deregulation that aided in the quick growth of the world's capital markets and a period of offshoring to benefit from the new supplies of cheap labor in the developing world. Further changes in international supply chains and cross-border e-commerce were also fueled by technology.

One possible result is that "giant's economic countries" may emerge to dominate the structure of the world economy in the twenty-first century. In addition to "giant" economies with sizable markets, such as the euro zone or the ASEAN Economic Community (AEC), which is the equivalent of the European

Union single market for the ten nations that make up the Association of Southeast Asian Nations (ASEAN), "giant" economies with sizable markets may increasingly drive global growth. These economies include China, India, and the United States. The tendency of combining markets to aid domestic businesses in achieving economies of scale is also being cited by the African Union and numerous organizations in Latin America. With many of the largest corporations in the world having their headquarters in "giant" economies and economic blocs, they would be better able to compete with them.

If this multipolar world develops well, the world economy may experience another era of prosperity. In the 1950s and 1960s, when there was peace and economic growth was at its peak, average salaries increased significantly. This expansion was fueled by the opening of US markets. When the US was the main driver of the strong expansion of the golden age, China's population was significantly larger than the US. The world's growth will probably be faster than it was when it was primarily driven by advanced economies, especially with rising economies like China, India, and Southeast Asia acting as engines. Because developing economies are in the process of industrializing or catching up, they grow more quickly than mature economies.

But it also implies that their growth paths are less steady and more erratic. Additionally, growth concentrated in such "giant" economic blocs presents difficulties for other nations. In order to compete and participate with "giant" economies that have populations over 100 million, nations would also need to think about their growth strategy. The growth of regional trade accords that aim to connect markets is already evidence of this. Most recently, the CPTPP, a free trade pact among 11 Asian economies that excludes the giants, the United States and China, was signed.

The issue for less populated countries would need to focus on how to compete, as well as integrate, in a global system with various poles of growth, given that the 21st century may see another "golden age" of prosperity driven by economies with huge numbers of middle class consumers. But it also means that smaller nations may be able to attach their economies to not just one, but numerous economic blocs to their advantage through the design of trade agreements and other types of global integration. Obviously, politics allowed.

In summary, the global economy of the twenty-first century is quite different from that of the twentieth. If billions of new middle class consumers from developing economies revitalized the global economy and ushered in yet another era of wealth, a new possible "golden age" may emerge. For a clearer understanding of how the structure of the globe has evolved, it will be crucial to observe how economies like China and other sizable markets are growing and reforming. Every country should take part in this effort.

2. Recommendations

-Every government should be able to catch up with modern technology and science. Since the first industrial revolution (first interviews in the 18th century in the United Kingdom), economic growth has depended so much on the capacity of states and nations to extract and harness natural resources, the capacity to innovate, the ability to produce, and the capacity to catch up with modern technology, as well as the ability to dominate the markets and the supply chains. Japan became the first industrialized country in Asia because of its ability to adopt Western technologies after and before the Second World War. China has had continuous growth for the last four decades and has become the world's largest economy because government policy has prioritized technology and science. The main factors of economic growth are technology, science, innovation, scientific research, manufacturing, productivity, and the ability to dominate markets. Therefore, the government and policymakers must be ready to adopt modern technology and science.

-Every nation should uphold international laws and contribute to sustainable and inclusive development. Human rights, freedoms, democracy, justice, the rule of law, and good governance are the main principles that every government has to obey. And no government can reject these fundamental principles. If these basic principles are not implemented, the government will face international criticism and opposition.

-The government should be able to express its abilities, its willingness, commitments, contributions, compassion, cooperation, morality, courage, character, and knowledge to contribute to solving the global crisis and being an active contributor to world peace and development. The world we are living in now is almost led by the media, modern technology, and information in social networks, and these things have great impacts on the whole society regarding reputation and recognition. So the state leader must be prudent and genuine in expressing its attitudes and characteristics toward other nations. Expressions of arrogance, violence, oppression, tyranny, and threatening behavior toward other nations will be considered serious violations of international laws. State leaders must demonstrate the commitments and contributions required to assist in resolving the international crisis of climate change, terrorism, extreme poverty, and willingness to comply with and adopt sustainable development goals, as well as willingness to uphold international laws and the international system.

-The state leaders and governments must work hard to promote the quality of education, social justice, and inclusive growth. Education quality is critical in eradicating extreme poverty, ending social injustice, promoting inclusive growth, ending social racism, ending domestic violence, closing the social gap, and promoting citizen equality. Furthermore, education is critical in advancing national economic growth, catching up with modern technology, promoting national innovation, and developing effective national living standards.

- Leaders and policymakers in every state must work together more to expand their markets and cooperation. A nation cannot depend on only a few business and trade partners and a few countries. Instead, a country should seek out cooperatives and broaden its global market. We are now living in a global system, which we have called globalization and multilateralism. So every state has the right to do business and become the trading partner of all countries without any oppression or coercion from any country. Every country has the ability to broaden its trading partners from Asia to Europe, North America to Central America, and America from west to east and north to south. For trading partners, there are no boundaries or barriers.

www.ingramcontent.com/pod-product-compliance
Lightning Source LLC
Chambersburg PA
CBHW031533210526
45464CB00014B/1917